DRAWING DRAPERY from HEAD to TOE

by *CLIFF YOUNG*

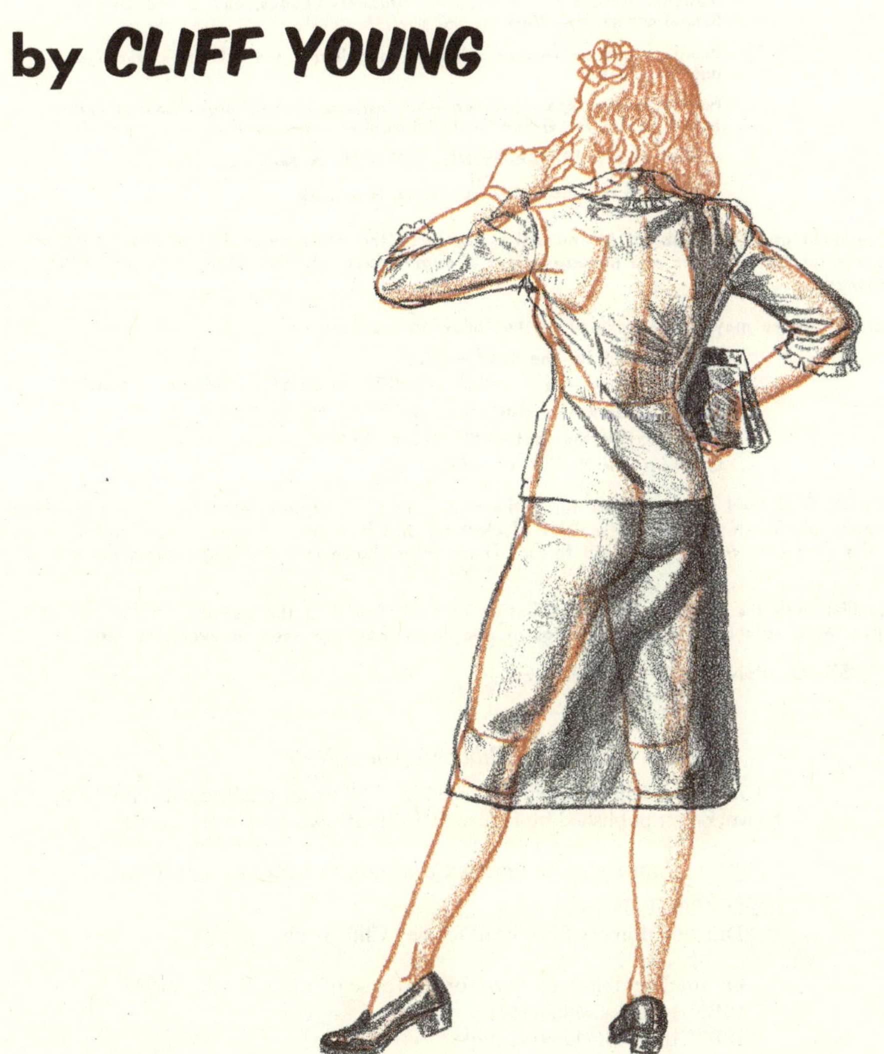

DOVER PUBLICATIONS, GARDEN CITY, NEW YORK

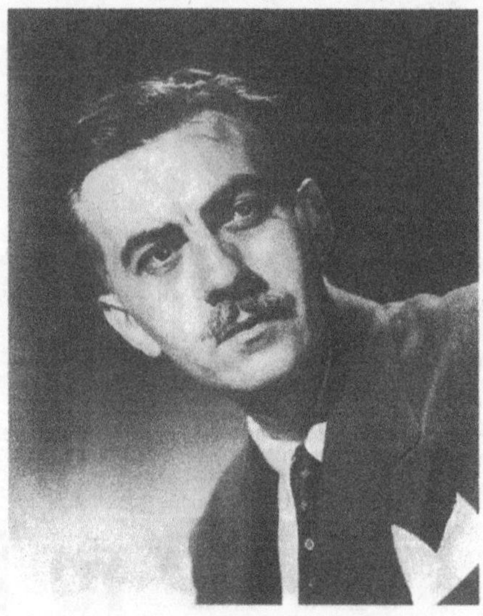

Photo by robert-scott studio

ABOUT THE AUTHOR

Studied at the Art Institute of Pittsburgh; Art Institute of Chicago; National Academy of Design, Art Students League, and Grand Central School of Art, New York.

Paintings and watercolors exhibited in galleries and exhibitions throughout the country.

Former lecturer and instructor,—Art Institute of Pittsburgh; Central Park School of Art, and Grand Central School of Art, New York.

Author of FIGURE DRAWING WITHOUT A MODEL.

Member of the Society of Illustrators, New York.

DRAPERY, a most important subject to the artist, has been the most neglected in the art school program. The study of the figure is, of course, basic and necessary, but in commercial art, illustration and portraiture you will rarely find the figure unclothed.

Drapery for the figure may be catalogued in the following manner:—

The covering for the head — HAT.
Drapery above the waistline — SHIRT, BLOUSE, COAT, or JACKET.
Drapery below the waistline — SKIRT or TROUSERS.
Covering for the feet — BOOTS or SHOES.
Covering for the hands — GLOVES.

When the body is clothed with all these items, the only part of the figure left uncovered is the face. You will readily see the importance of the study of these articles of clothing and how they drape on the figure. An action, however slight, will cause the garments worn to fall into folds. These folds shown in a drawing explain the action of the figure enclosed by clothing.

Become familiar with the sources and the radiation of folds found in the various articles of clothing and use this knowledge to give more authority to your drawings of people as they are seen in everyday life.

BE AN ARTIST—DESIGN YOUR KNOWLEDGE.

Bibliographical Note

This Dover edition, first published in 2007, is an unabridged republication of the work first published by House of Little Books, New York, in 1947.

Library of Congress Cataloging-in-Publication Data

Young, Cliff, 1905–
Drawing drapery from head to toe / Cliff Young.
p. cm.
Originally published: New York : House of Little Books, c1947.
ISBN-13: 978-0-486-45591-4 (pbk.)
ISBN-10: 0-486-45591-2 (pbk.)
1. Drapery in art. 2. Human figure in art. 3. Drawing—Technique. I. Title.

NC775.Y6 2007
743.4—dc22

2006053477

Printed in Canada
45591210 2025
www.doverpublications.com

Progress step by step from the study of cloth and the draping of a single piece of material to the physical appearance of clothing on the figure at rest and in action. The classifications below will assist you in your studies.

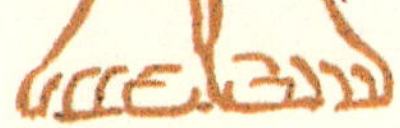

FROM CLOTH . . .

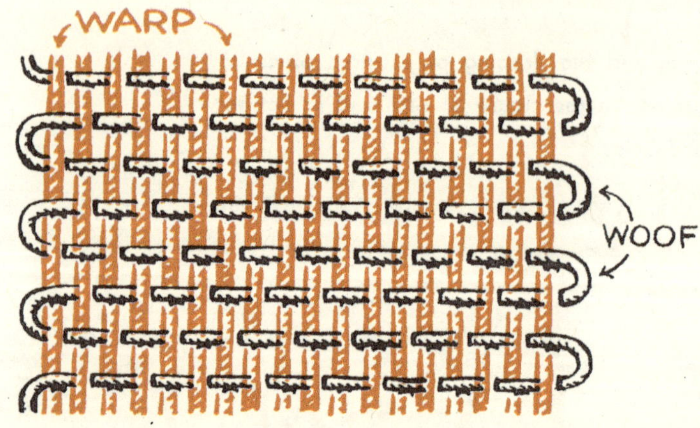

Drapery is cloth. You must know what cloth is.

Cloth is made of threads woven together as shown in the illustration to the left. The threads may be of wool, cotton, silk, etc.

The length-wise threads, as shown in red, are called the WARP. The threads which are woven back and forth by the shuttle in the making of fabrics are known as the WOOF. These are the black threads shown in the illustrations to the left.

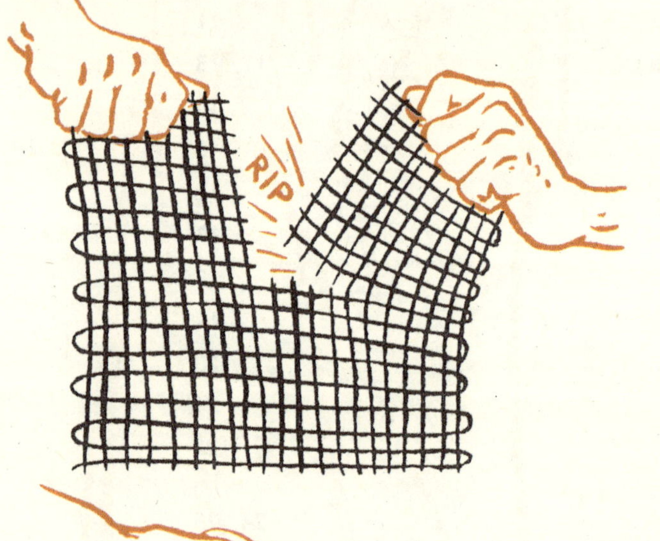

When cloth is torn the threads of the WARP or the WOOF are broken. See the illustration to the left. It is impossible to tear cloth diagonally. When a change in direction occurs in a tear, it is always at right angles to the WARP or WOOF.

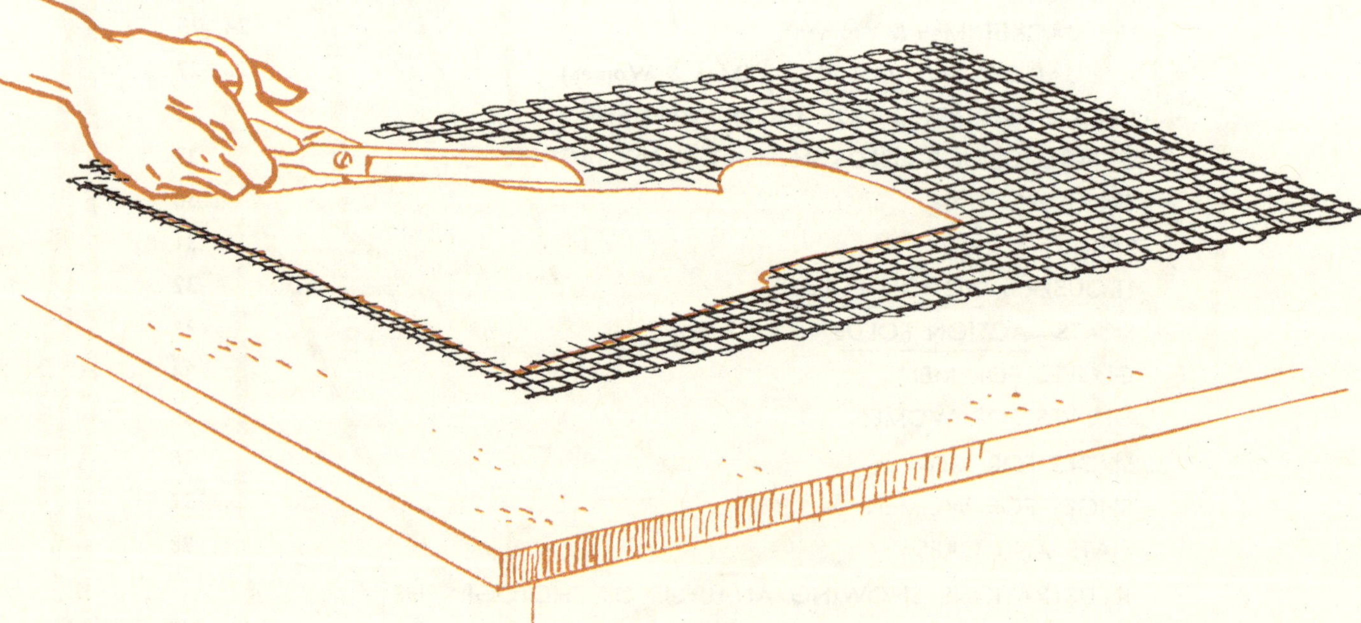

If it is necessary to have cloth of irregular shapes, the cloth must be cut to shape with a pair of scissors. The illustration above shows a paper pattern laid on cloth as a guide to cutting. These facts are known to all, but it is well to recall them to mind in order that you may know the nature of the material with which clothing is made.

• • • TO CLOTHES

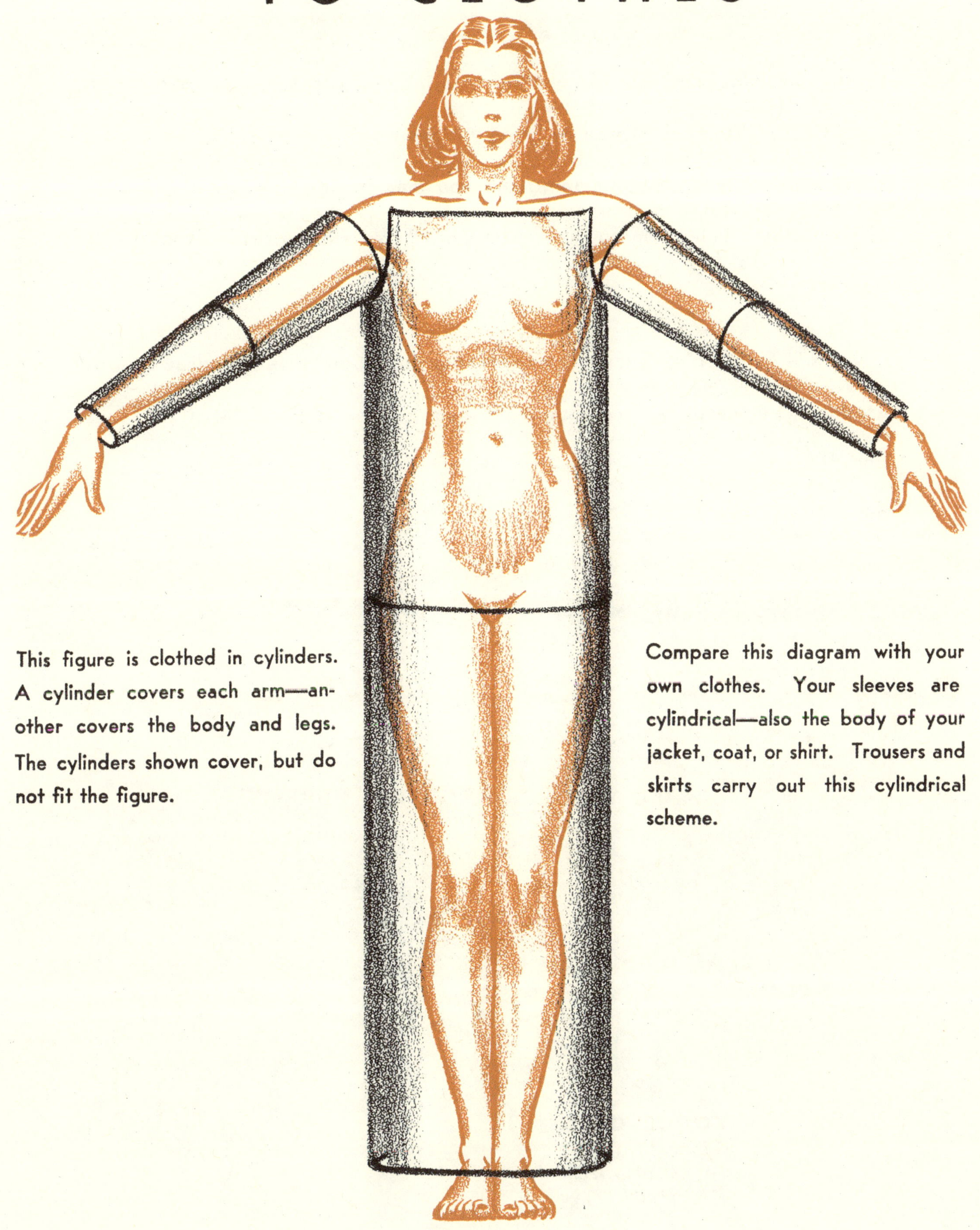

This figure is clothed in cylinders. A cylinder covers each arm—another covers the body and legs. The cylinders shown cover, but do not fit the figure.

Compare this diagram with your own clothes. Your sleeves are cylindrical—also the body of your jacket, coat, or shirt. Trousers and skirts carry out this cylindrical scheme.

DRAPERY

Clothes are simply pieces of cloth sewn together to make a covering for the nude figure. Study the force of gravity (downward pull) on one piece of cloth under many conditions. By doing this you may better understand the cause of the folds which seem to give so much trouble when drawing the clothed figure.

If you will take a piece of cloth a yard square and make various drawing of it, as shown by the drawings on the following pages, you will learn the cause and formation of folds which add interest to an otherwise plain piece of material.

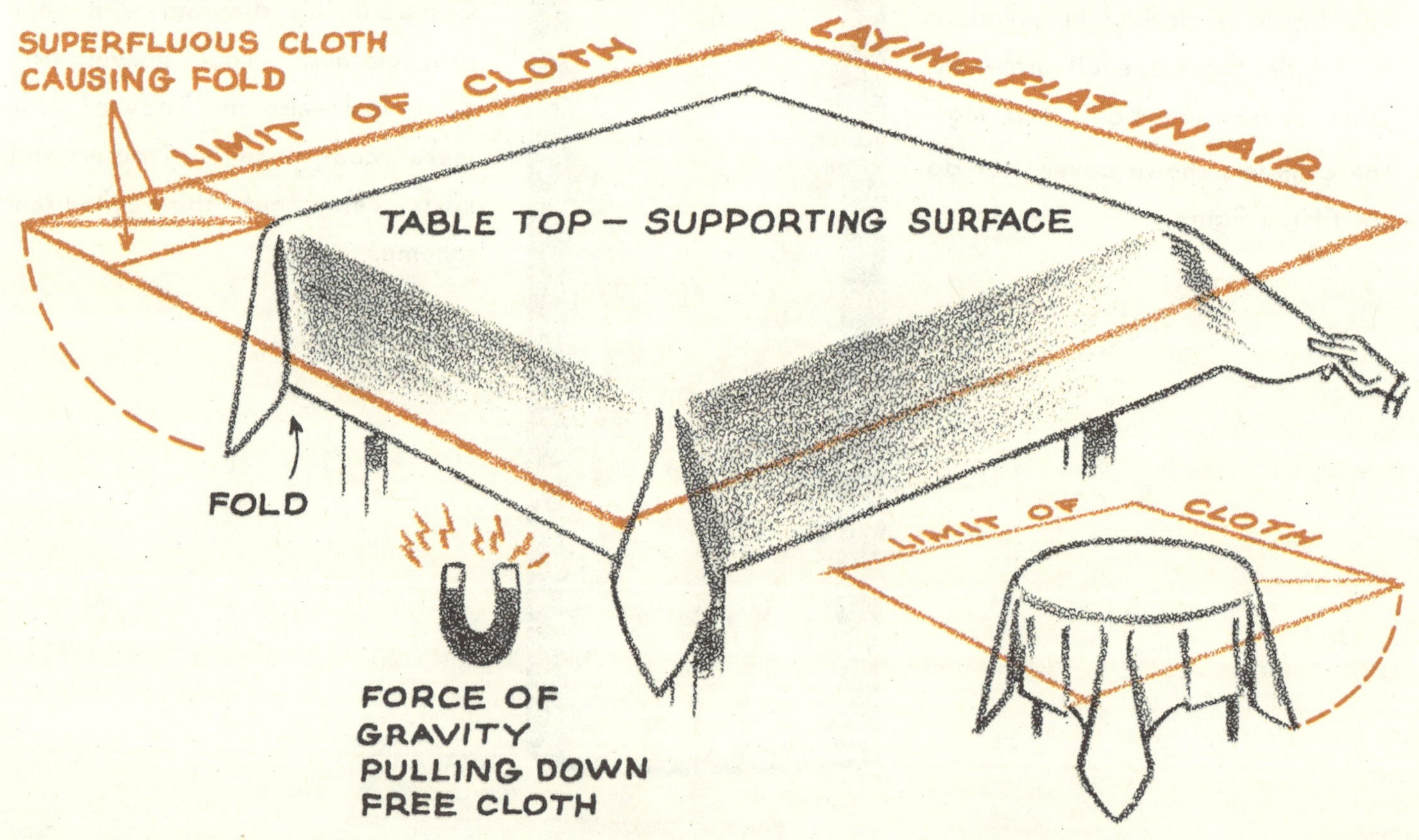

DRAPERY IN ACTION

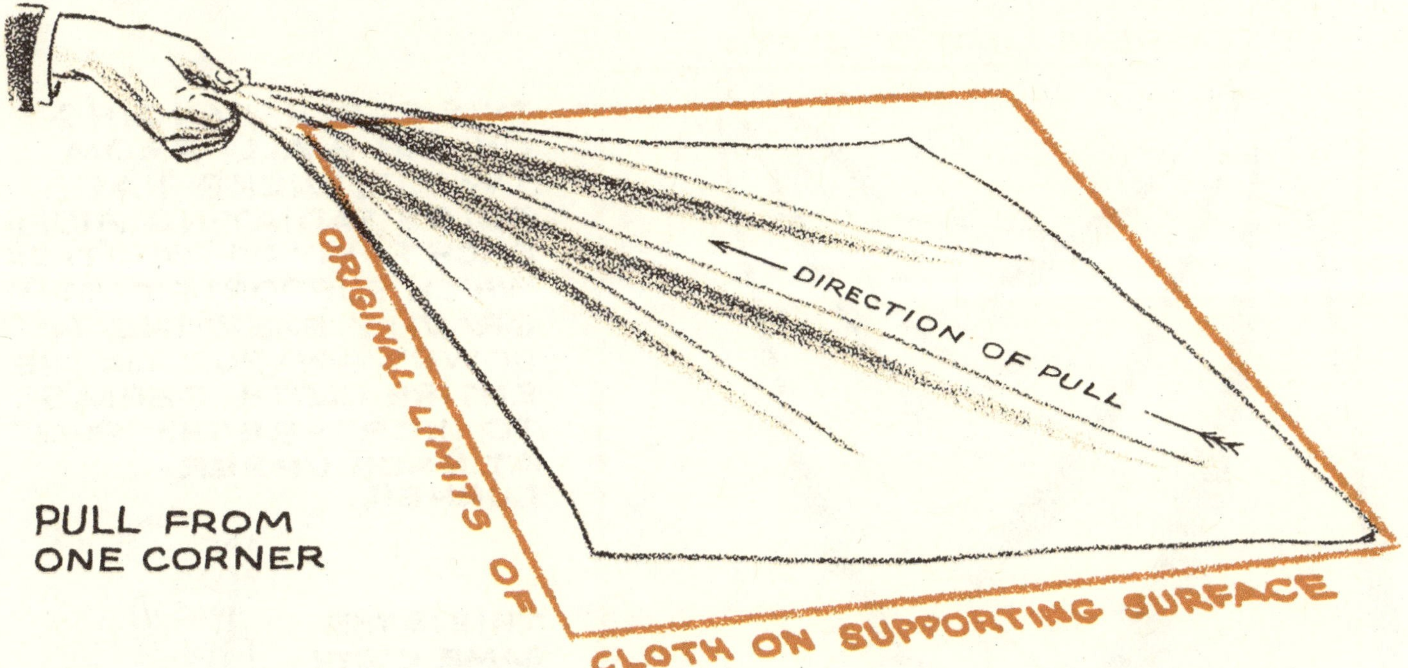

A CLOTH LAID FLAT ON THE FLOOR AND PULLED FROM ONE CORNER WILL CAUSE FOLDS TO RADIATE FROM THIS POINT OF *PULL*.

WHEN THE CLOTH IS PULLED AT TWO CORNERS AT THE SAME TIME FOLDS WILL RADIATE FROM BOTH POINTS OF *PULL*. TRY IT AND SEE.

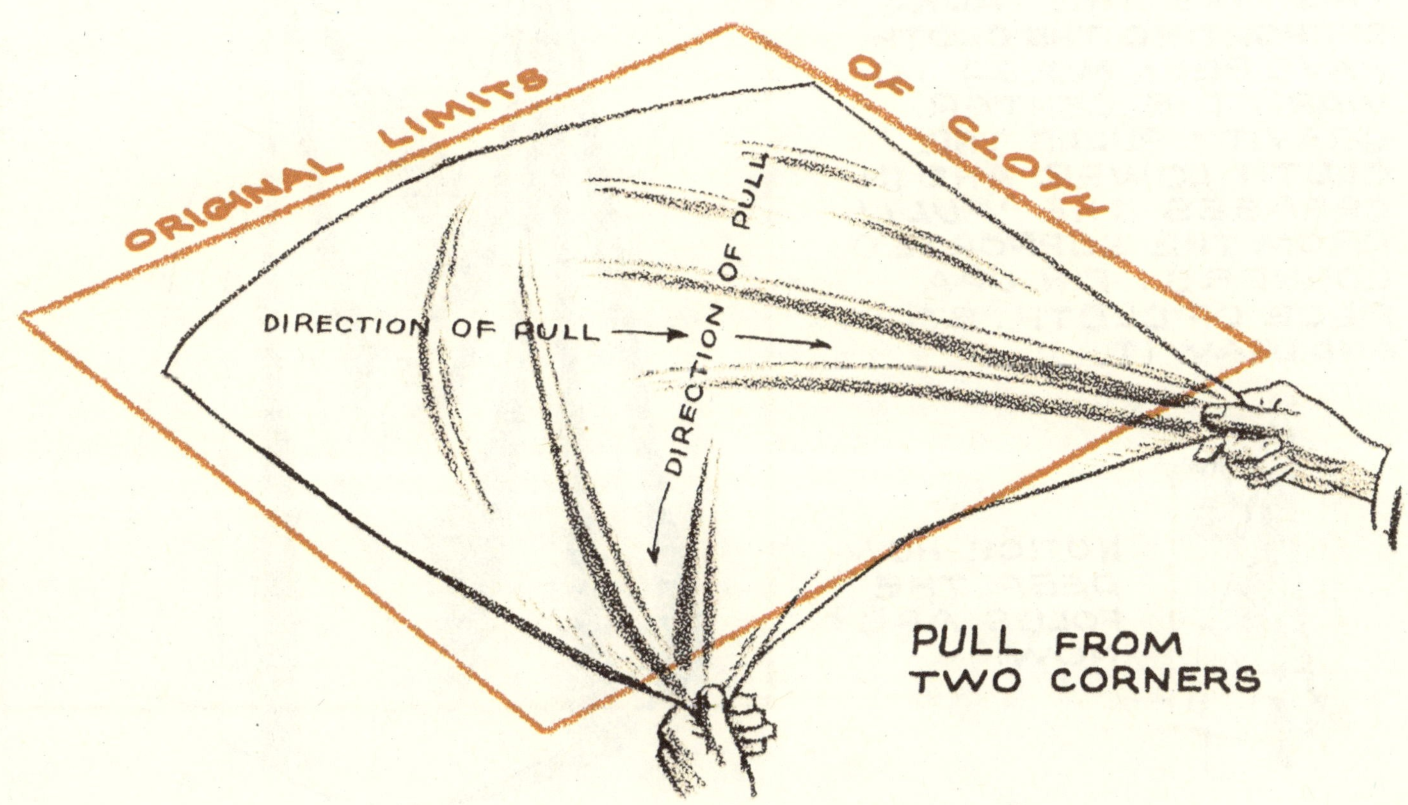

THE INFLUENCE OF . . .

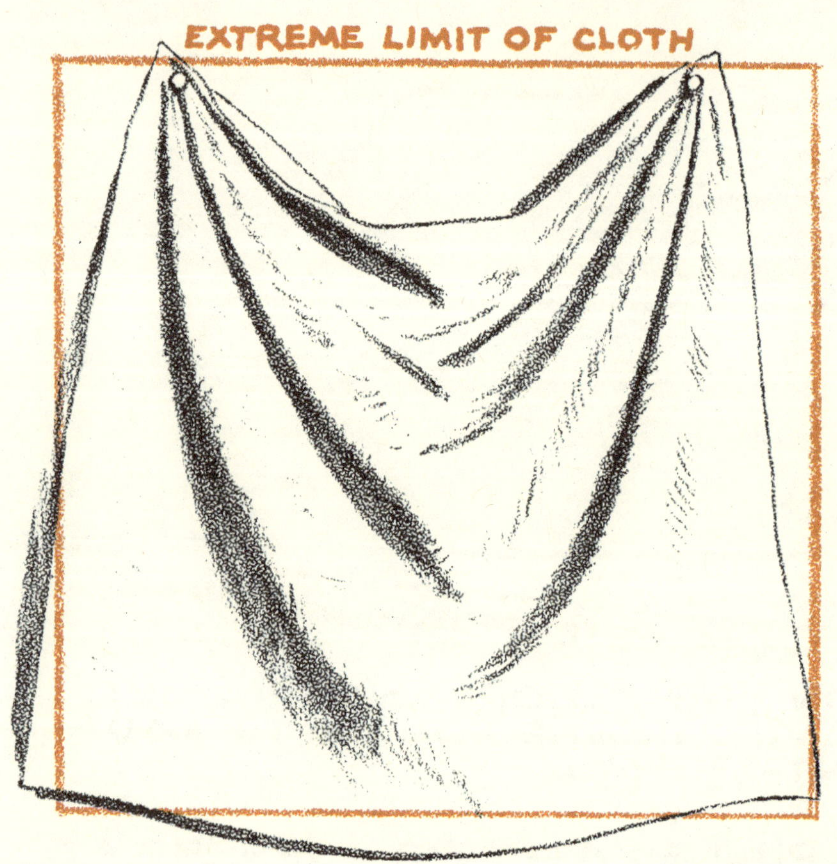

THIS CLOTH HANGING ON THE WALL FROM TWO CORNERS HAS FOLDS RADIATING FROM EACH POINT OF *PULL* (TACK WHICH SUPPORTS CLOTH). GRAVITY, EXERTING A DOWNWARD PULL ON THE ENTIRE CLOTH, SEEMS TO INCREASE THE '*PULL*' AT EACH UPPER CORNER.

THIS IS THE SAME CLOTH SEEN FROM THE SIDE →

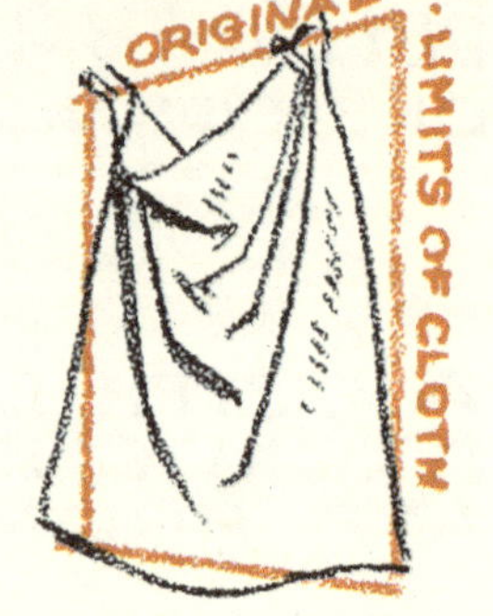

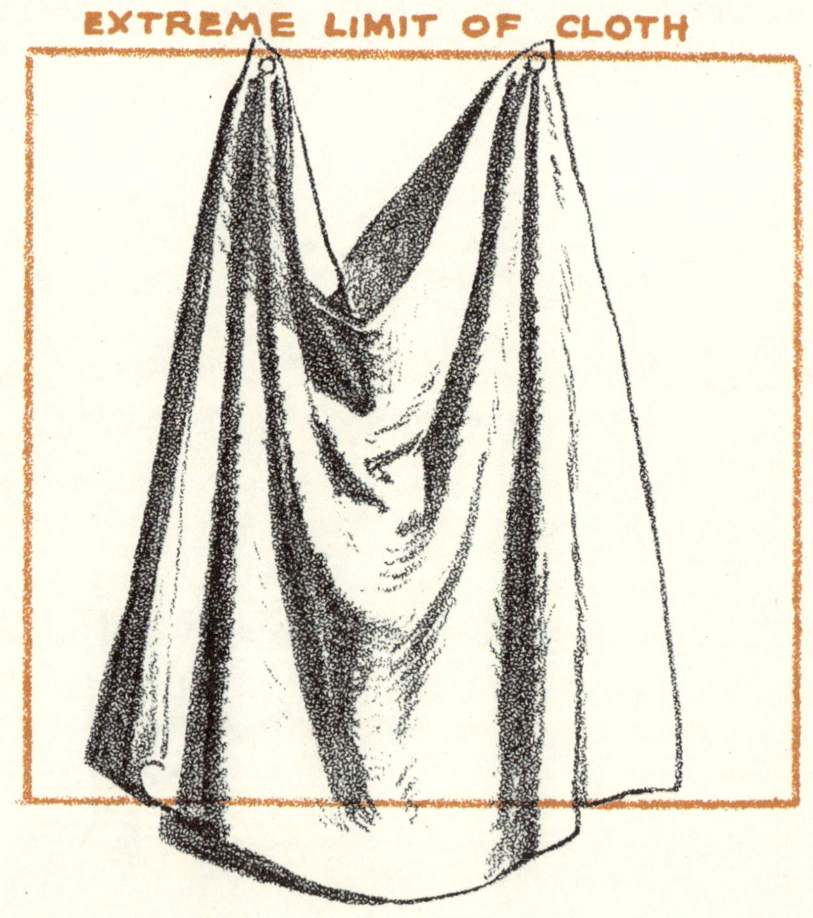

THIS TIME THE TACKS SUPPORTING THE CLOTH HAVE BEEN MOVED TO-WARD THE CENTER. GRAVITY PULLS THE CLOTH LOWER AND IN-CREASES THE '*PULL*' FROM THE SUPPORTED CORNERS. PIN UP A PIECE OF CLOTH. STUDY AND DRAW IT.

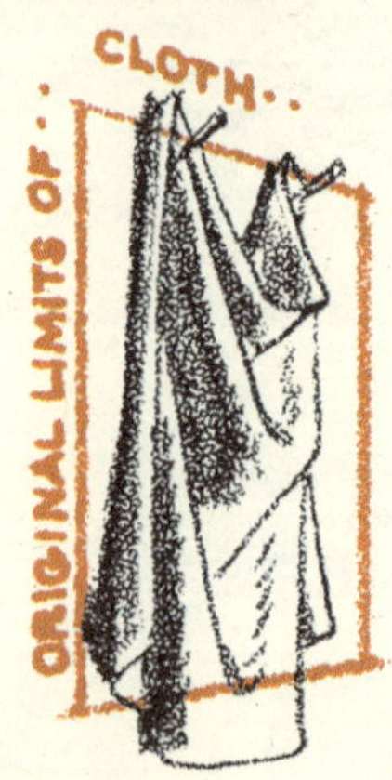

NOTICE HOW *DEEP* THE FOLDS ARE NOW.

GRAVITY ON DRAPERY

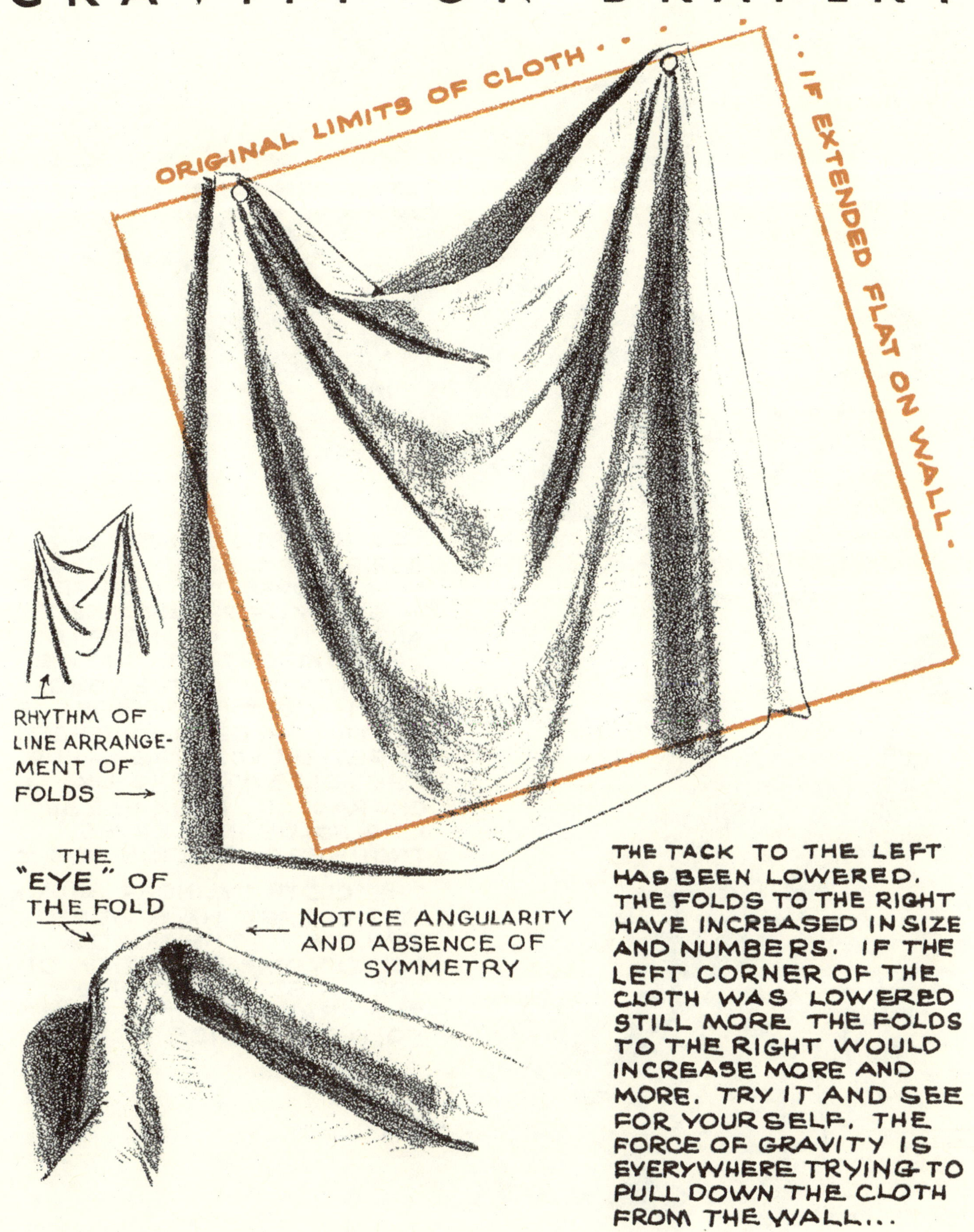

THE TACK TO THE LEFT HAS BEEN LOWERED. THE FOLDS TO THE RIGHT HAVE INCREASED IN SIZE AND NUMBERS. IF THE LEFT CORNER OF THE CLOTH WAS LOWERED STILL MORE THE FOLDS TO THE RIGHT WOULD INCREASE MORE AND MORE. TRY IT AND SEE FOR YOURSELF. THE FORCE OF GRAVITY IS EVERYWHERE TRYING TO PULL DOWN THE CLOTH FROM THE WALL...

CRUSHED CYLINDERS

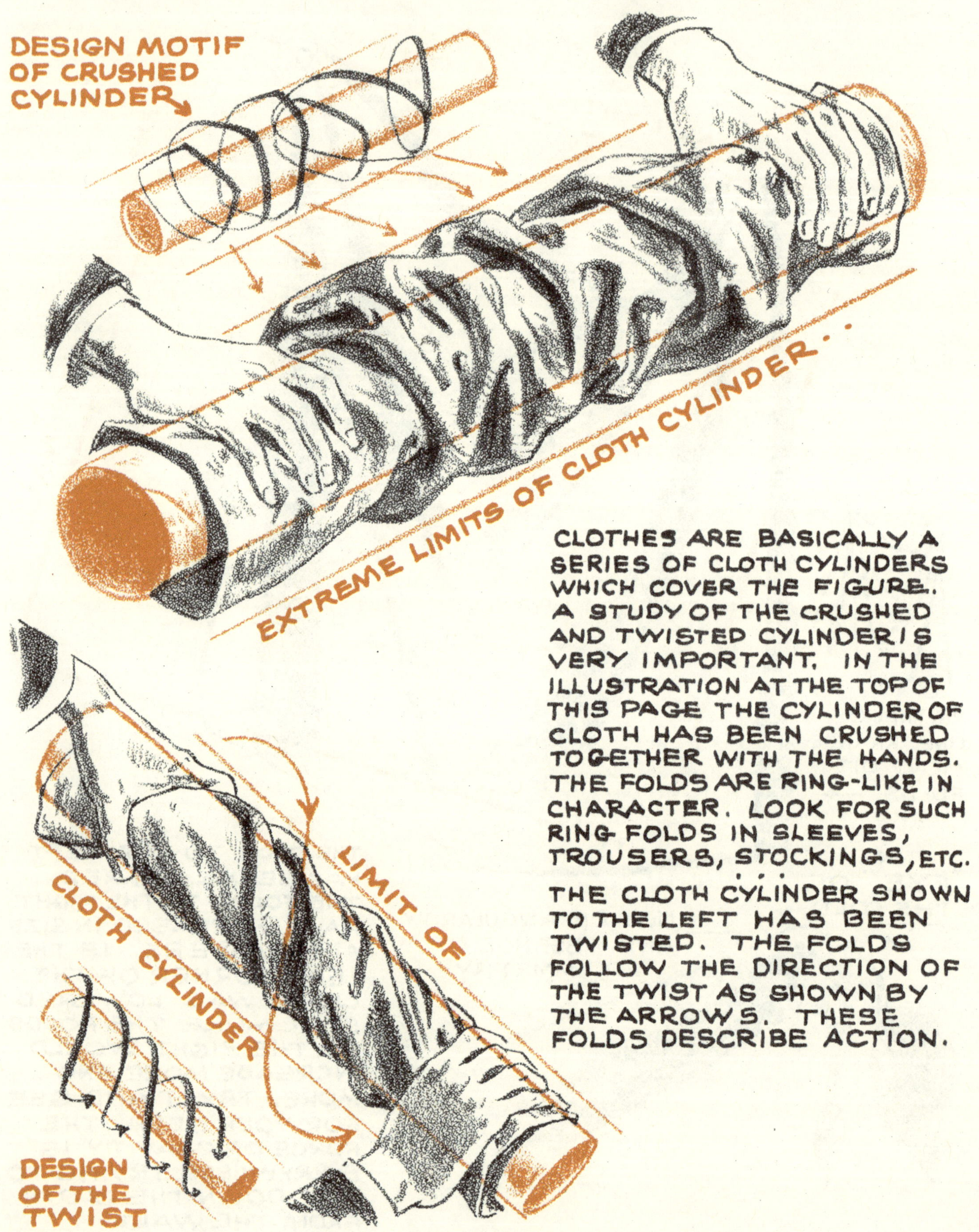

CLOTHES ARE BASICALLY A SERIES OF CLOTH CYLINDERS WHICH COVER THE FIGURE. A STUDY OF THE CRUSHED AND TWISTED CYLINDER IS VERY IMPORTANT. IN THE ILLUSTRATION AT THE TOP OF THIS PAGE THE CYLINDER OF CLOTH HAS BEEN CRUSHED TOGETHER WITH THE HANDS. THE FOLDS ARE RING-LIKE IN CHARACTER. LOOK FOR SUCH RING FOLDS IN SLEEVES, TROUSERS, STOCKINGS, ETC.

. . .

THE CLOTH CYLINDER SHOWN TO THE LEFT HAS BEEN TWISTED. THE FOLDS FOLLOW THE DIRECTION OF THE TWIST AS SHOWN BY THE ARROWS. THESE FOLDS DESCRIBE ACTION.

BENT CYLINDERS

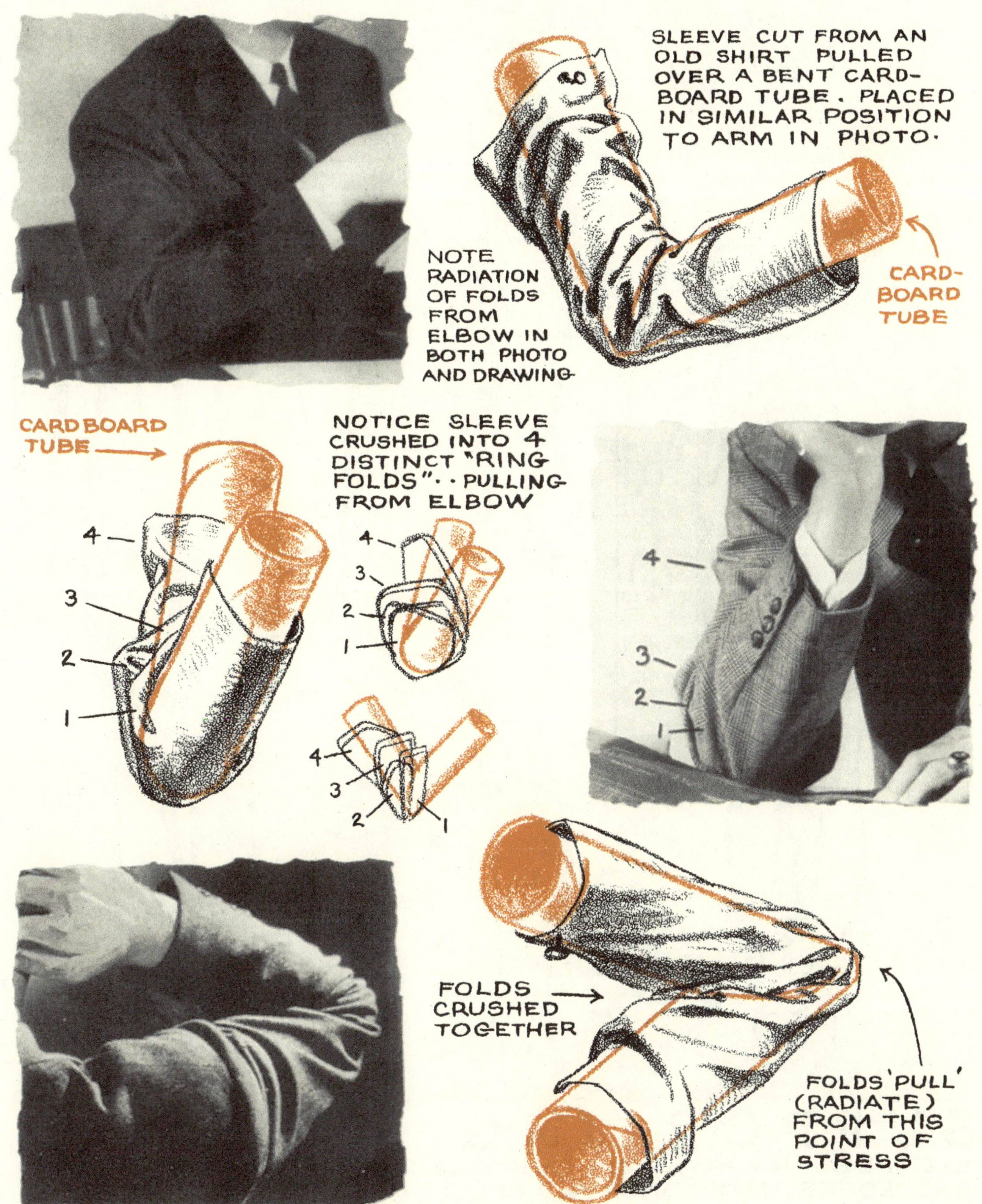

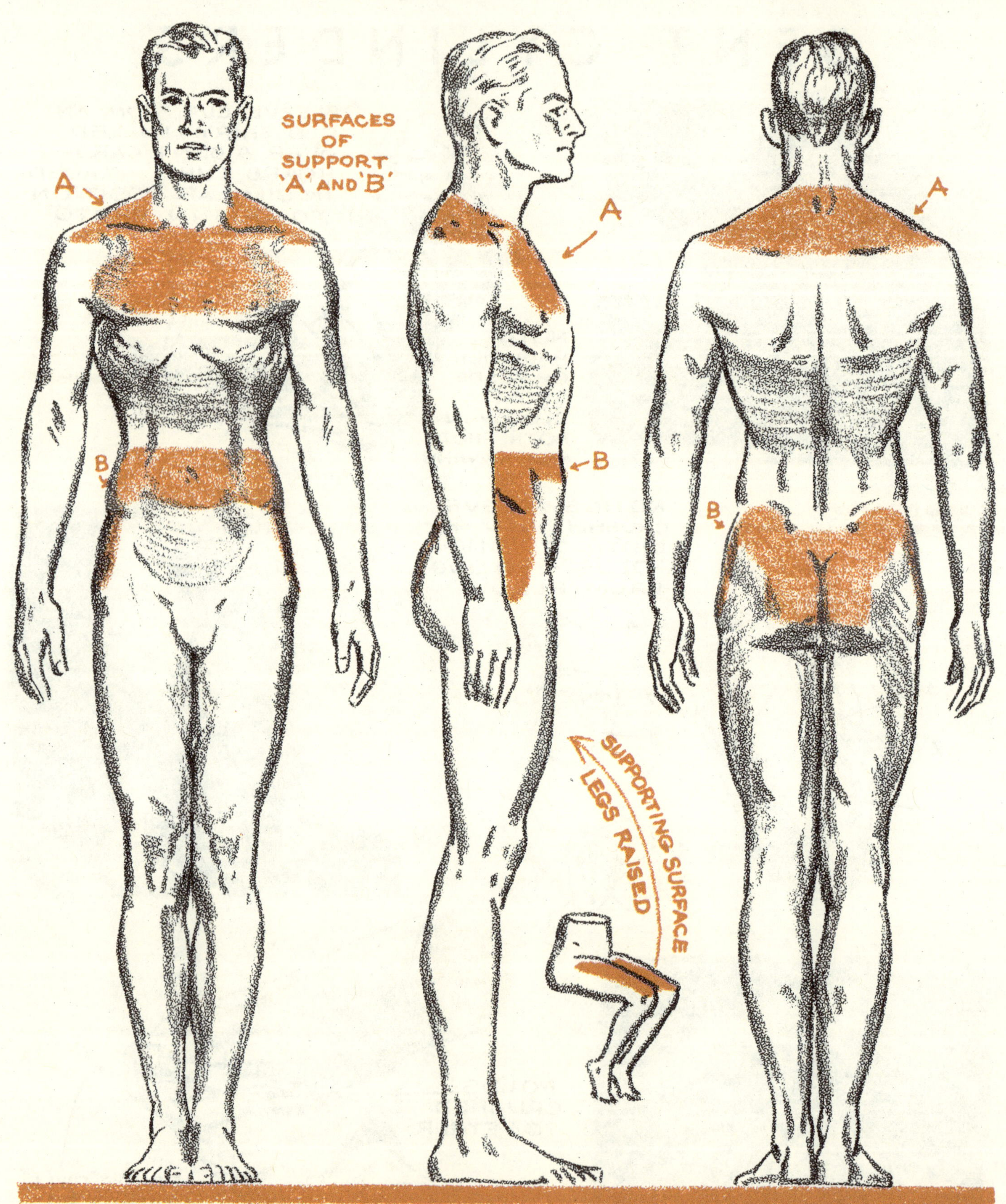

SUPPORTING SURFACES

CLOTHES ARE HUNG ON SUPPORTING SURFACES... THE SHOULDERS, UPPER BACK AND CHEST (A) SUPPORT CLOTHING THAT COVERS THE UPPER PART OF THE BODY.

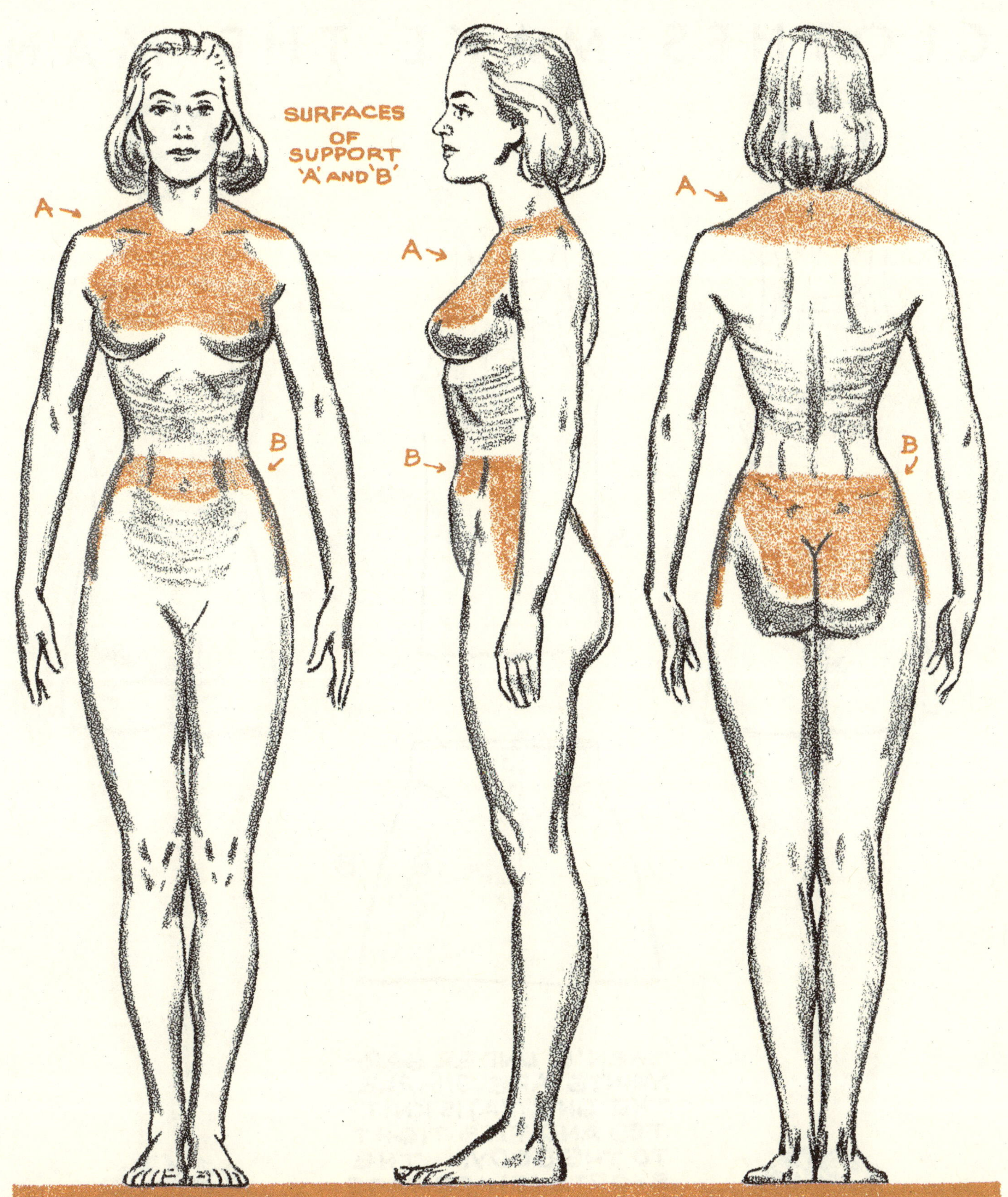

SUPPORTING SURFACES

THE HIPS AND BUTTOCKS (B) SUPPORT THE CLOTHING COVERING THE LOWER PART OF THE FIGURE. NOTICE INCREASE OF SUPPORTING SURFACE CAUSED BY THE PROJECTION OF BREASTS.

CLOTHES MAKE THE MAN

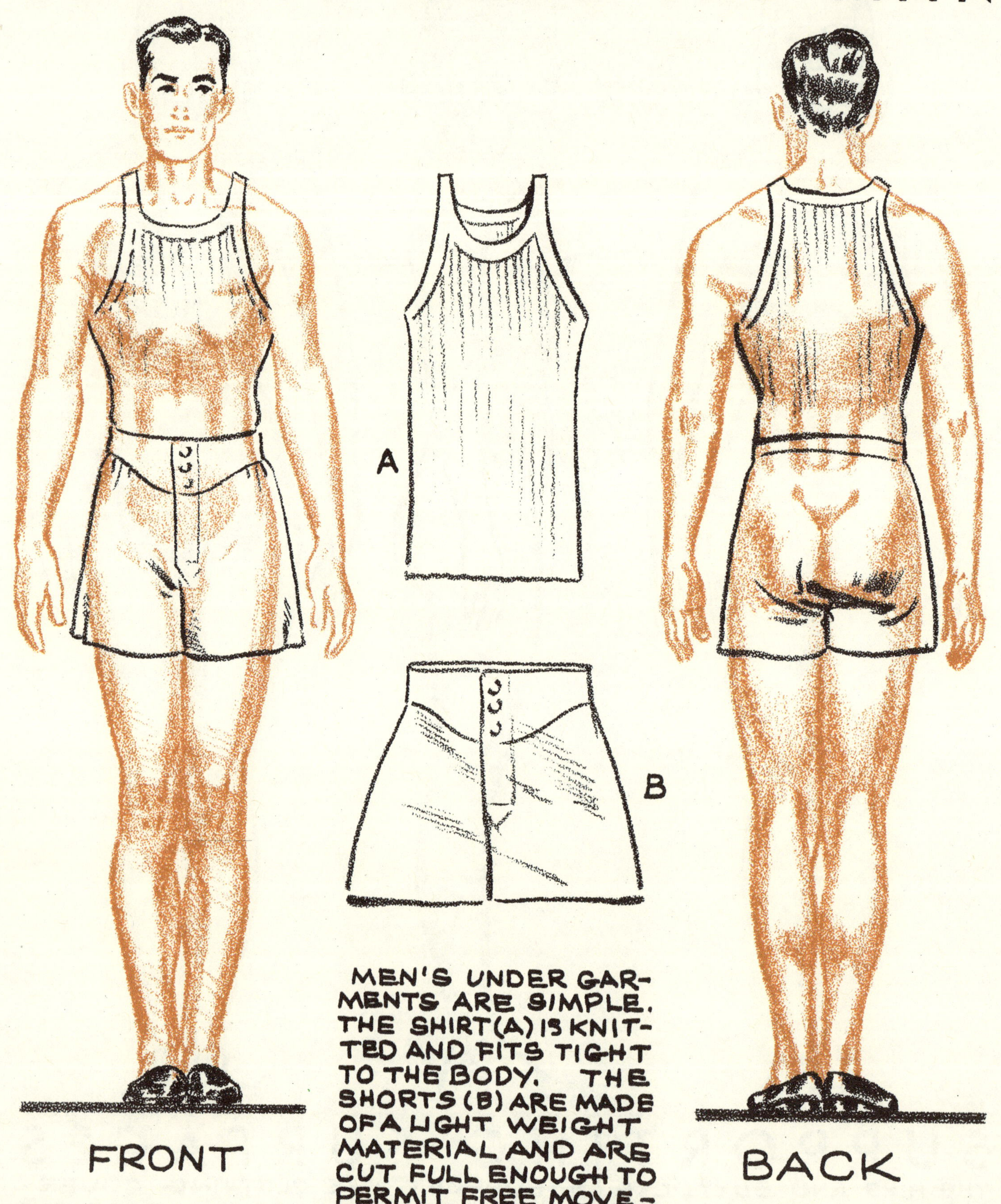

MEN'S UNDER GARMENTS ARE SIMPLE. THE SHIRT (A) IS KNITTED AND FITS TIGHT TO THE BODY. THE SHORTS (B) ARE MADE OF A LIGHT WEIGHT MATERIAL AND ARE CUT FULL ENOUGH TO PERMIT FREE MOVEMENT OF THE LEGS.

. . . . . . AND THE WOMAN

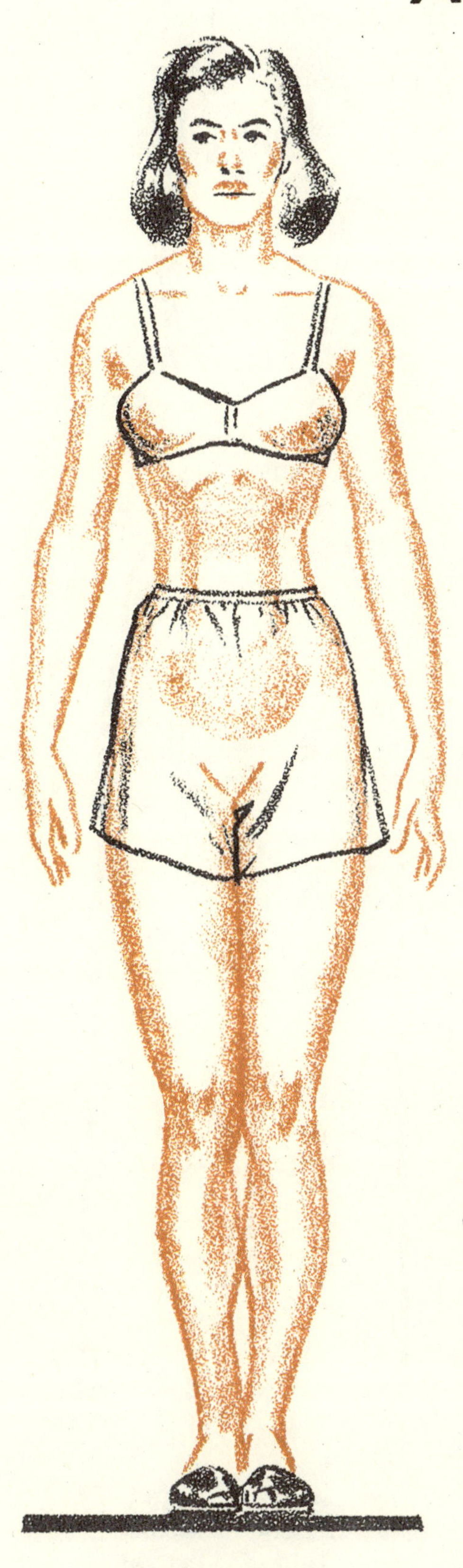

FRONT

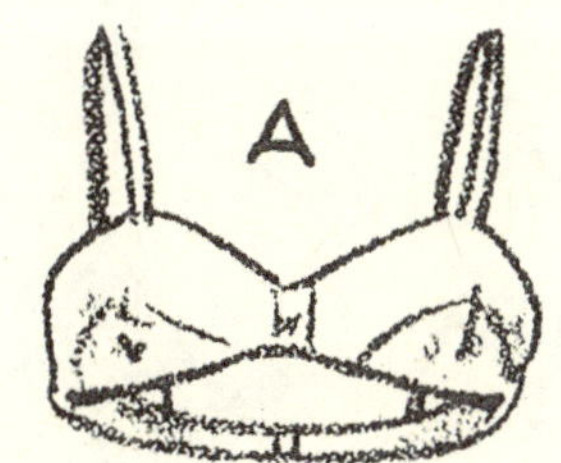

A

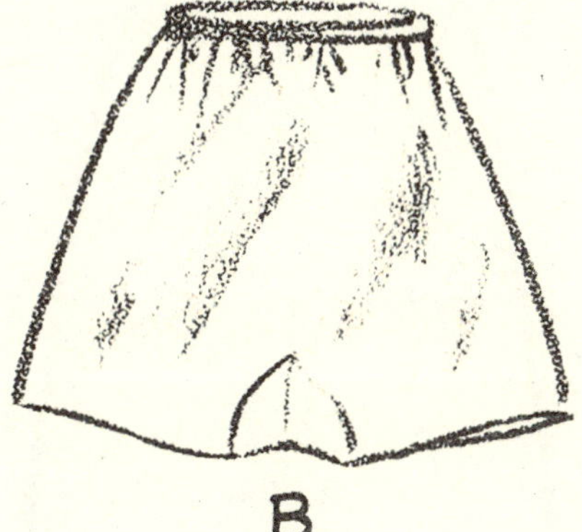

B

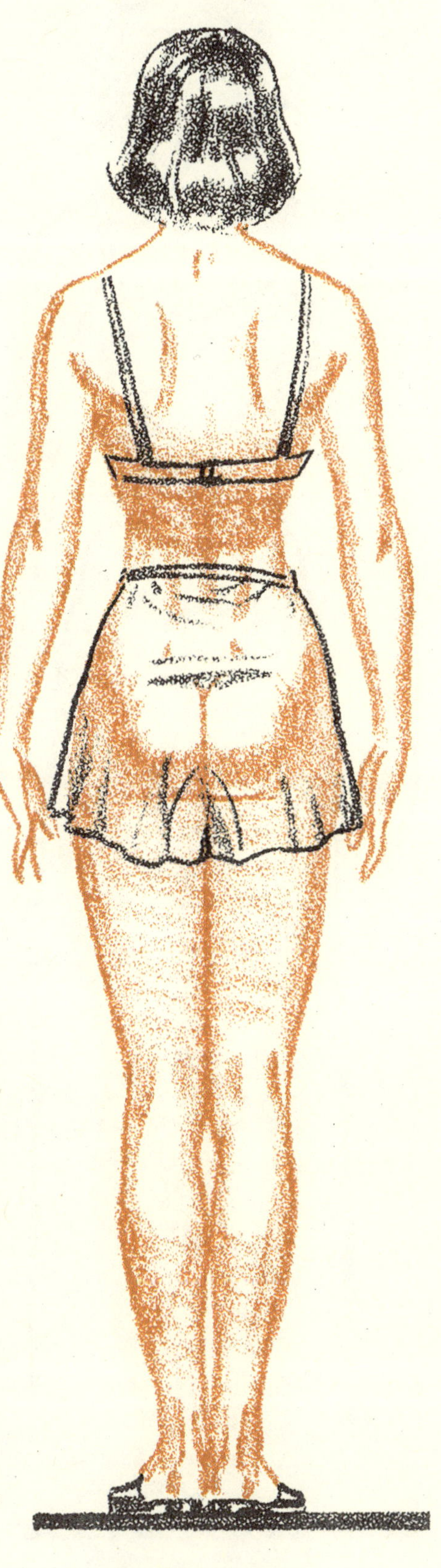

BACK

THERE IS MUCH VARIETY IN THE STYLE OF WOMEN'S CLOTHING. THE 'BRASSIERE' (A), A COVERING AND PROTECTION FOR THE BREASTS, AND THE 'PANTIES' (B), ARE WORN NEXT TO THE SKIN. FOUNDATION GARMENTS OVER WHICH THE OTHER ARTICLES OF CLOTHING ARE WORN. MAILORDER CATALOGS AND ADVERTISING PHOTOS IN MAGAZINES ARE A GOOD SOURCE OF INFORMATION FOR THE MANY STYLES OF CLOTHING...

SLIPS

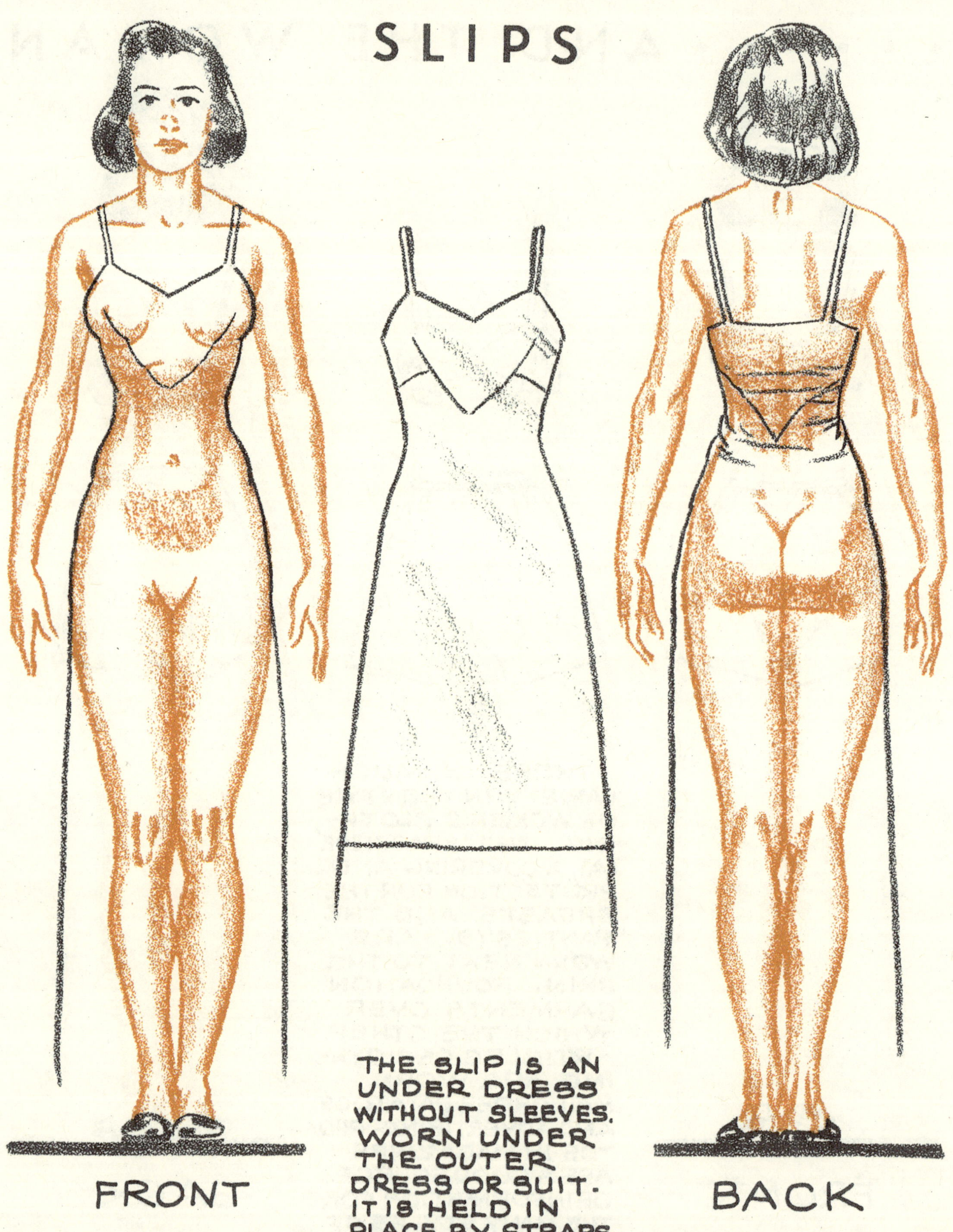

THE SLIP IS AN UNDER DRESS WITHOUT SLEEVES. WORN UNDER THE OUTER DRESS OR SUIT. IT IS HELD IN PLACE BY STRAPS OVER THE SHOULDERS

NIGHT CLOTHES

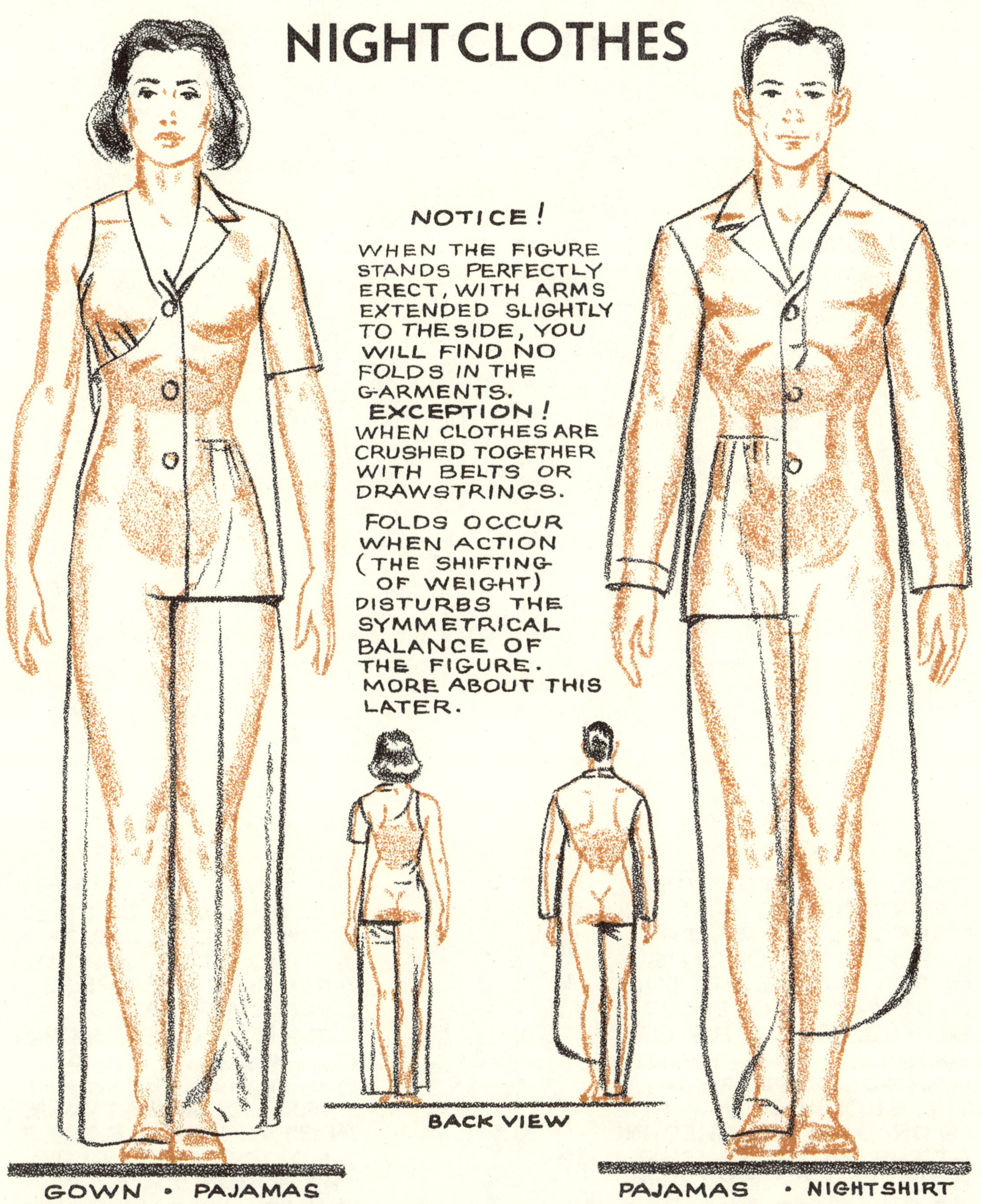

GOWN • PAJAMAS

PAJAMAS • NIGHTSHIRT

THE GOWN AND NIGHTSHIRT IS A NIGHT DRESS. THE PAJAMA IS A TWO PIECE GARMENT. A SLEEPING SUIT.. SEE FASHION MAGAZINES AND CATALOGS FOR STYLES....

THE SHIRT

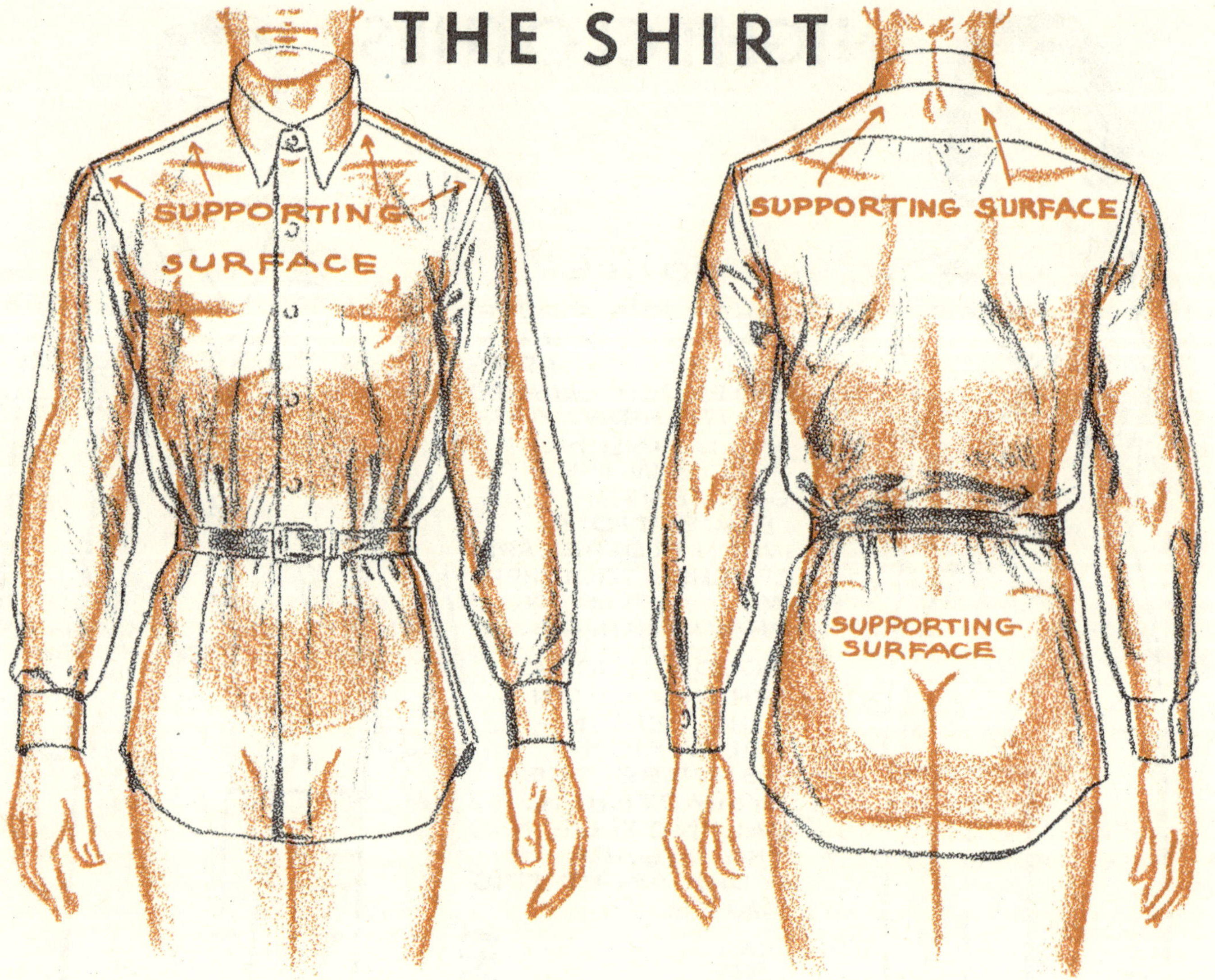

SUPPORTING SURFACE

SUPPORTING SURFACE

SUPPORTING SURFACE

THE SHIRT, THE FIRST OF THE OUTER GARMENTS, COVERS THE UPPER PART OF THE BODY. THE SHIRT TAIL IS USUALLY COVERED BY THE TROUSERS OR SKIRT. THE SHIRT HANGS LOOSE FROM THE SHOULDERS. IT IS DRAWN (CRUSHED) IN AT THE WAIST BY THE BELT (TOP OF TROUSERS OR SKIRT). FOLDS CAUSED BY THE BELT CRUSHING THE LOOSE SHIRT ARE SIMILAR TO THE ONES PRODUCED BY THE STRING TIED TIGHTLY AROUND A PAPER CYLINDER (A)

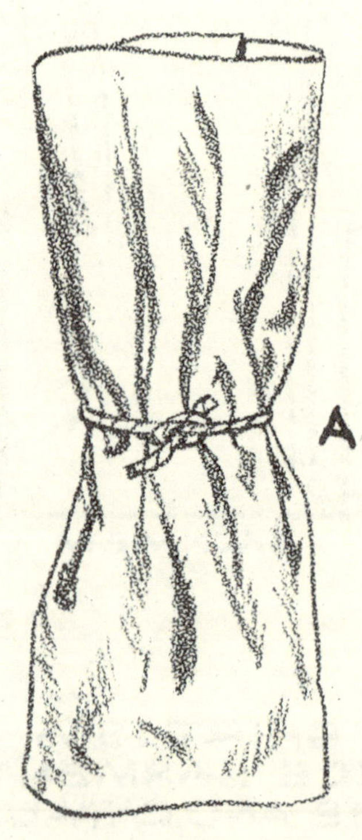

THE BLOUSE SHOWN ON PAGE 19 IS A SHIRT WORN BY WOMEN. THERE IS GREAT VARIETY IN STYLE OF SLEEVES AND COLLARS. ALSO THE SHIRT TAIL IS SHORT. LOOK ABOUT YOU. NOTICE STYLE.

THE BLOUSE

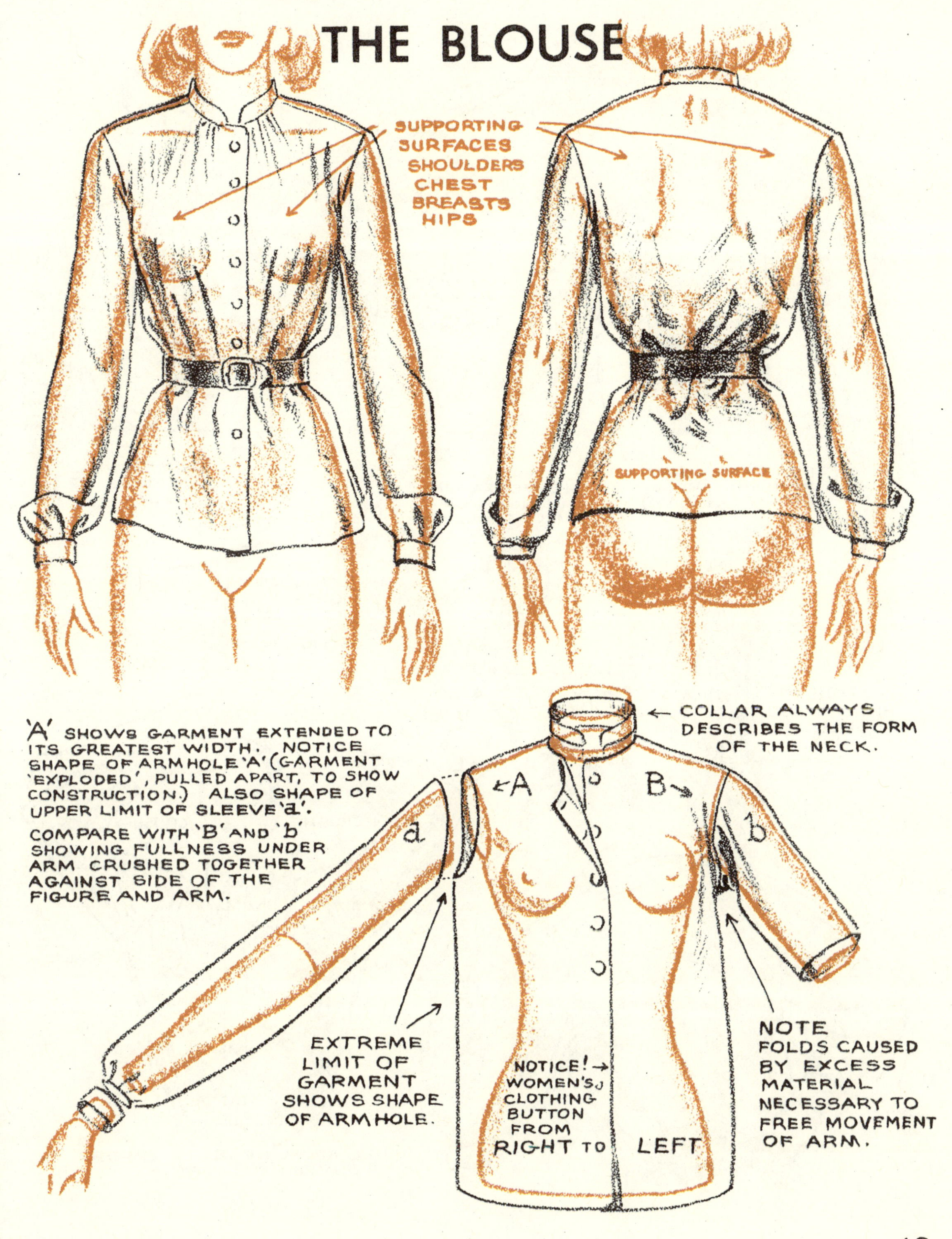
SUPPORTING SURFACES
SHOULDERS
CHEST
BREASTS
HIPS
SUPPORTING SURFACE
'A' SHOWS GARMENT EXTENDED TO ITS GREATEST WIDTH. NOTICE SHAPE OF ARMHOLE 'A' (GARMENT 'EXPLODED', PULLED APART, TO SHOW CONSTRUCTION.) ALSO SHAPE OF UPPER LIMIT OF SLEEVE 'a'.
COMPARE WITH 'B' AND 'b' SHOWING FULLNESS UNDER ARM CRUSHED TOGETHER AGAINST SIDE OF THE FIGURE AND ARM.
← COLLAR ALWAYS DESCRIBES THE FORM OF THE NECK.
A
B
a
b
EXTREME LIMIT OF GARMENT SHOWS SHAPE OF ARMHOLE.
NOTICE! → WOMEN'S CLOTHING BUTTON FROM RIGHT TO LEFT
NOTE FOLDS CAUSED BY EXCESS MATERIAL NECESSARY TO FREE MOVEMENT OF ARM.

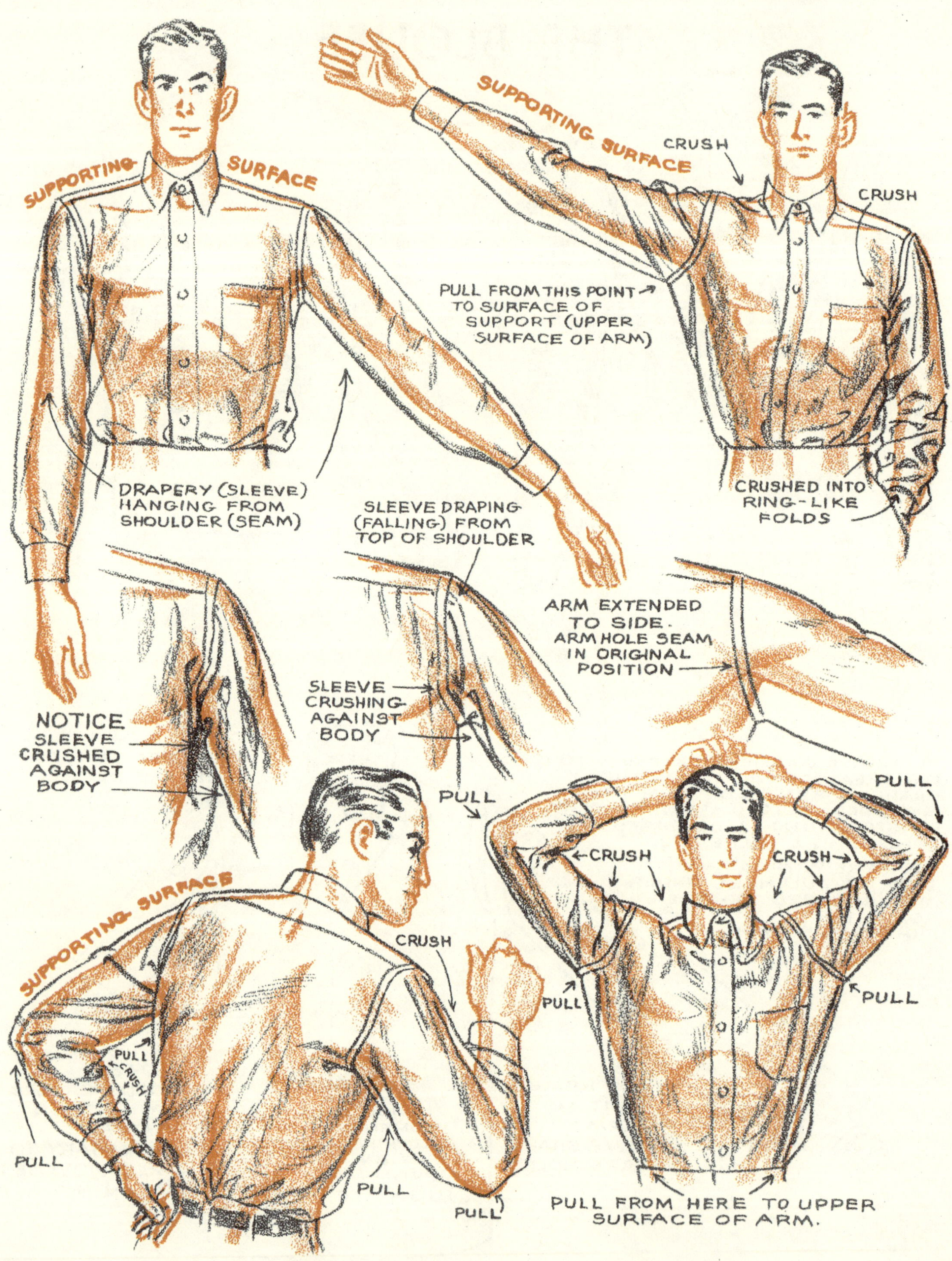
SUPPORTING SURFACE
DRAPERY (SLEEVE) HANGING FROM SHOULDER (SEAM)
SUPPORTING SURFACE
CRUSH
CRUSH
PULL FROM THIS POINT TO SURFACE OF SUPPORT (UPPER SURFACE OF ARM)
CRUSHED INTO RING-LIKE FOLDS
SLEEVE DRAPING (FALLING) FROM TOP OF SHOULDER
ARM EXTENDED TO SIDE. ARM HOLE SEAM IN ORIGINAL POSITION
NOTICE SLEEVE CRUSHED AGAINST BODY
SLEEVE CRUSHING AGAINST BODY
PULL
PULL
CRUSH
CRUSH
PULL
PULL
SUPPORTING SURFACE
CRUSH
PULL
CRUSH
PULL
PULL
PULL
PULL FROM HERE TO UPPER SURFACE OF ARM.

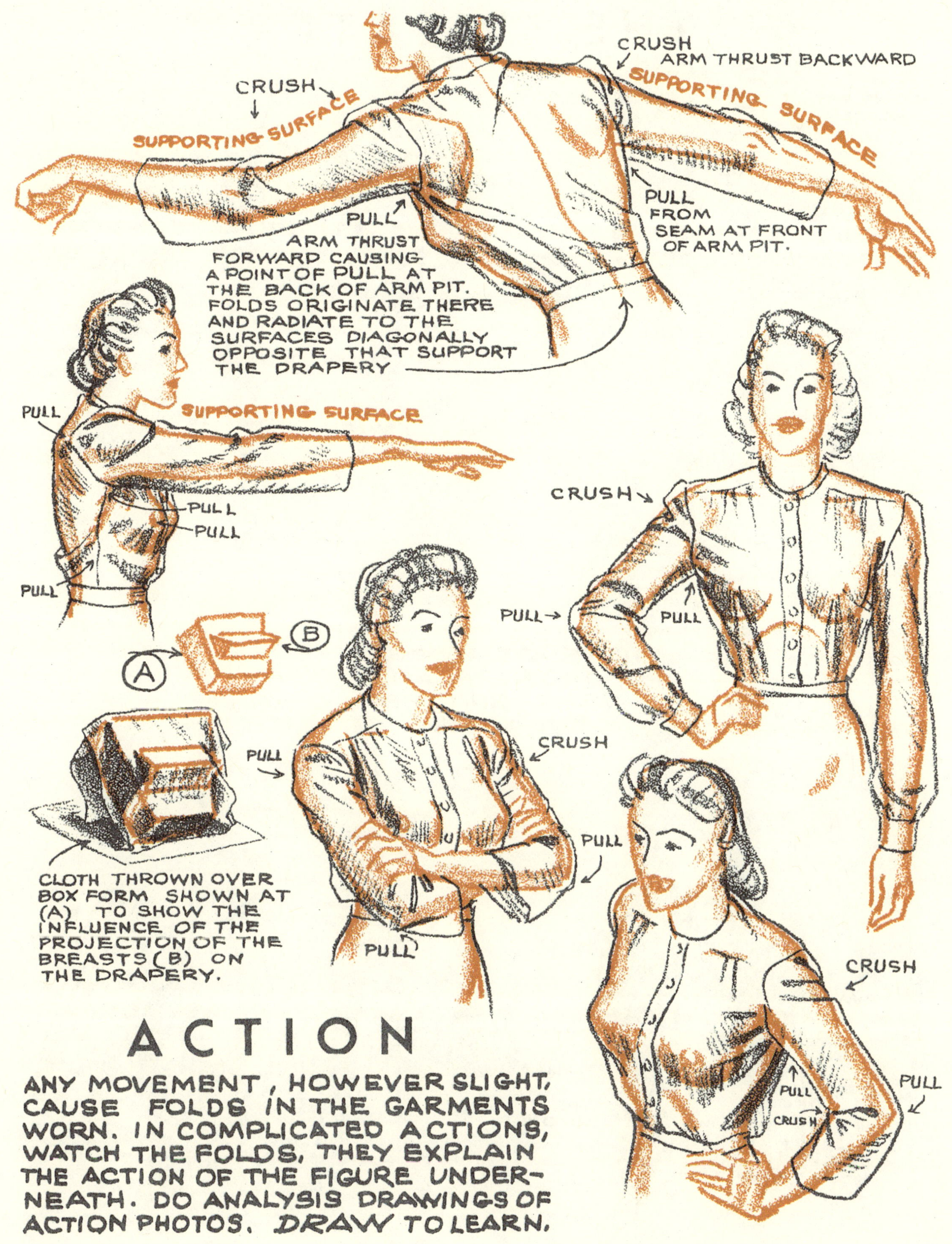

ACTION

ANY MOVEMENT, HOWEVER SLIGHT, CAUSE FOLDS IN THE GARMENTS WORN. IN COMPLICATED ACTIONS, WATCH THE FOLDS, THEY EXPLAIN THE ACTION OF THE FIGURE UNDERNEATH. DO ANALYSIS DRAWINGS OF ACTION PHOTOS. *DRAW* TO LEARN.

THE SWEATER

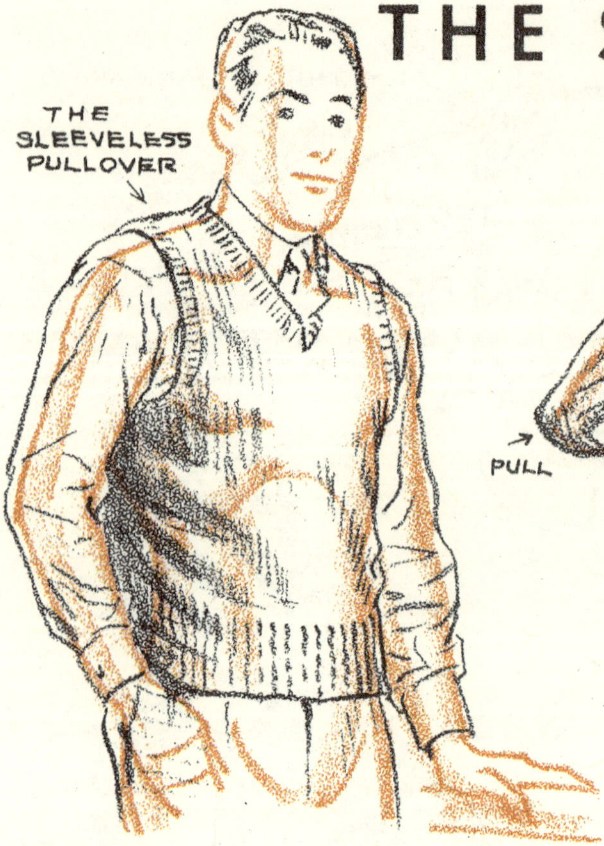

THE SLEEVELESS PULLOVER

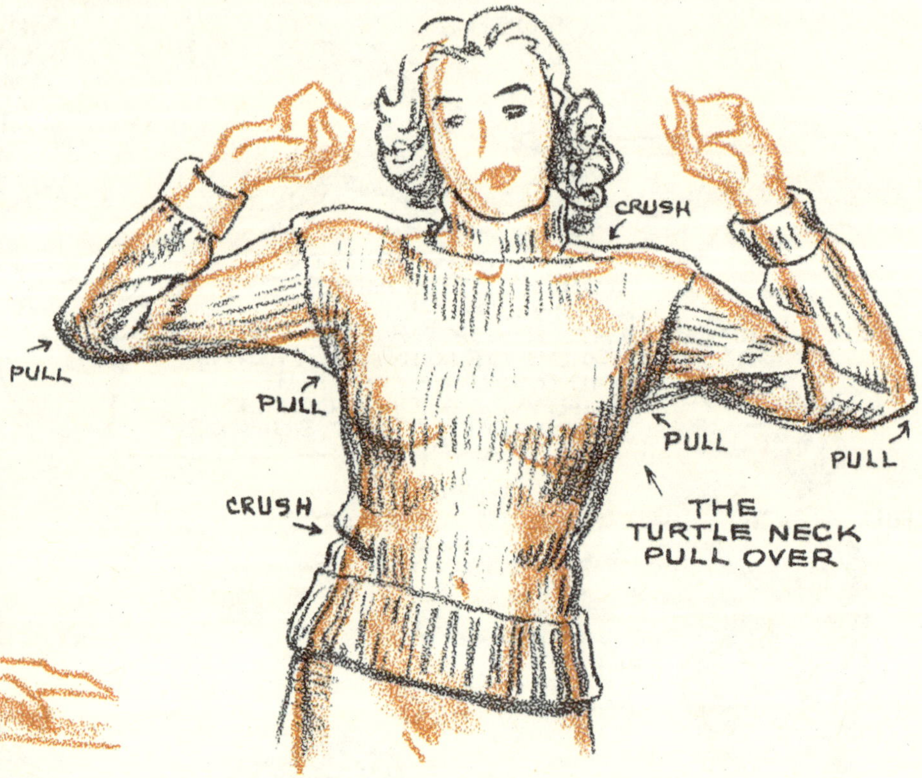

CRUSH

PULL

PULL

PULL

PULL

CRUSH

THE TURTLE NECK PULL OVER

HERE ARE A FEW OF THE POPULAR TYPES OF KNITTED SWEATERS.

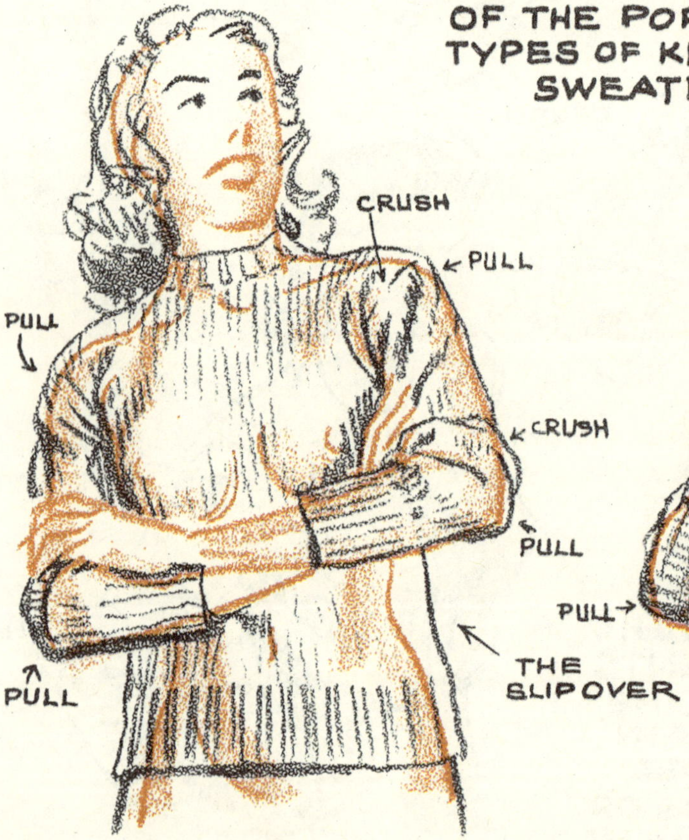

CRUSH

PULL

PULL

CRUSH

PULL

PULL

THE SLIPOVER

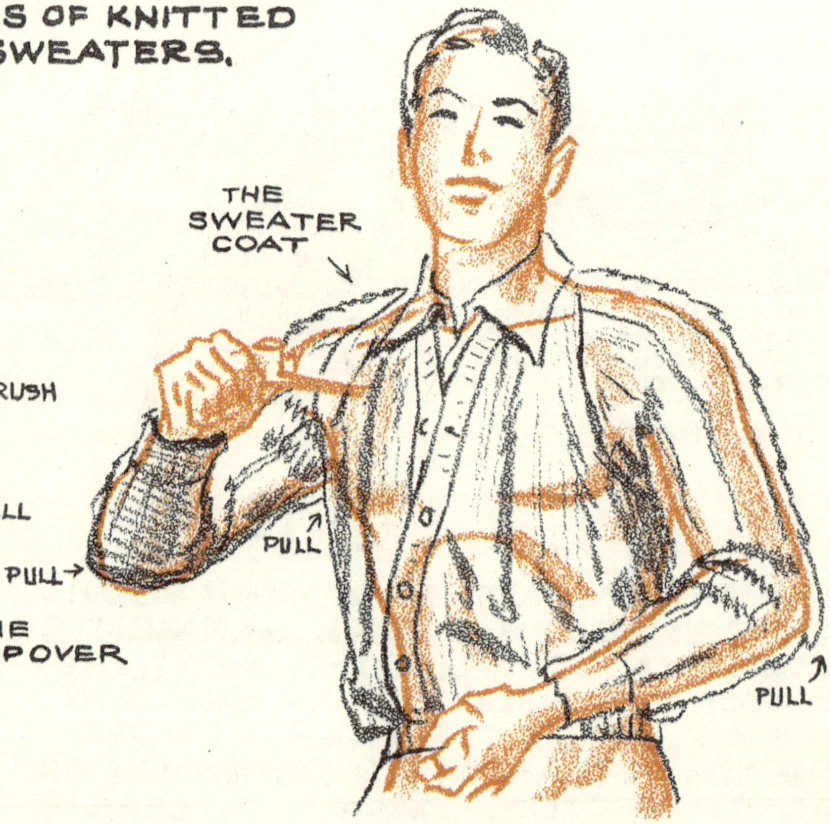

THE SWEATER COAT

PULL

PULL

PULL

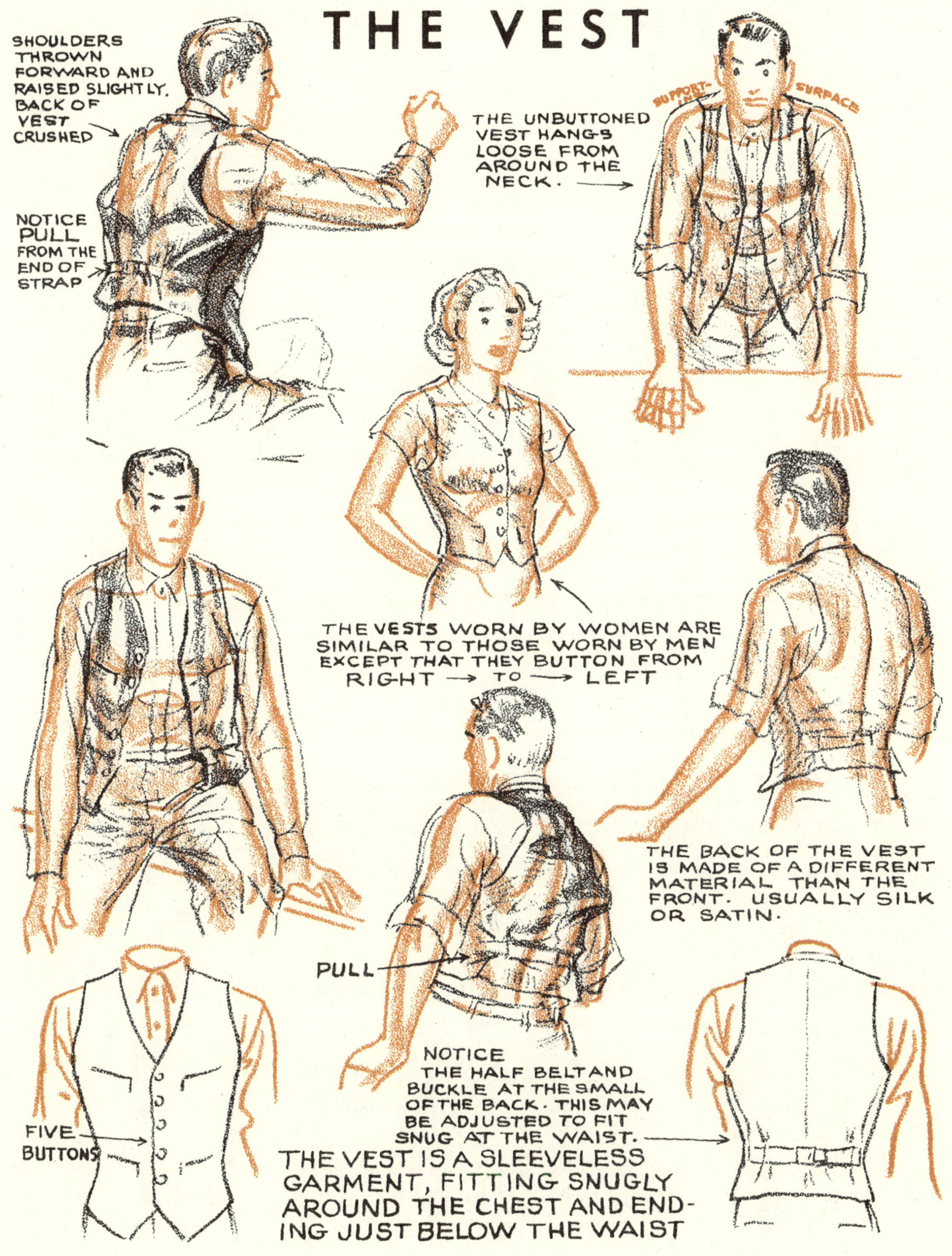
THE VEST
SHOULDERS THROWN FORWARD AND RAISED SLIGHTLY. BACK OF VEST CRUSHED
NOTICE PULL FROM THE END OF STRAP
THE UNBUTTONED VEST HANGS LOOSE FROM AROUND THE NECK.
THE VESTS WORN BY WOMEN ARE SIMILAR TO THOSE WORN BY MEN EXCEPT THAT THEY BUTTON FROM RIGHT → TO → LEFT
THE BACK OF THE VEST IS MADE OF A DIFFERENT MATERIAL THAN THE FRONT. USUALLY SILK OR SATIN.
PULL
FIVE BUTTONS
NOTICE THE HALF BELT AND BUCKLE AT THE SMALL OF THE BACK. THIS MAY BE ADJUSTED TO FIT SNUG AT THE WAIST.
THE VEST IS A SLEEVELESS GARMENT, FITTING SNUGLY AROUND THE CHEST AND ENDING JUST BELOW THE WAIST

THE JACKET

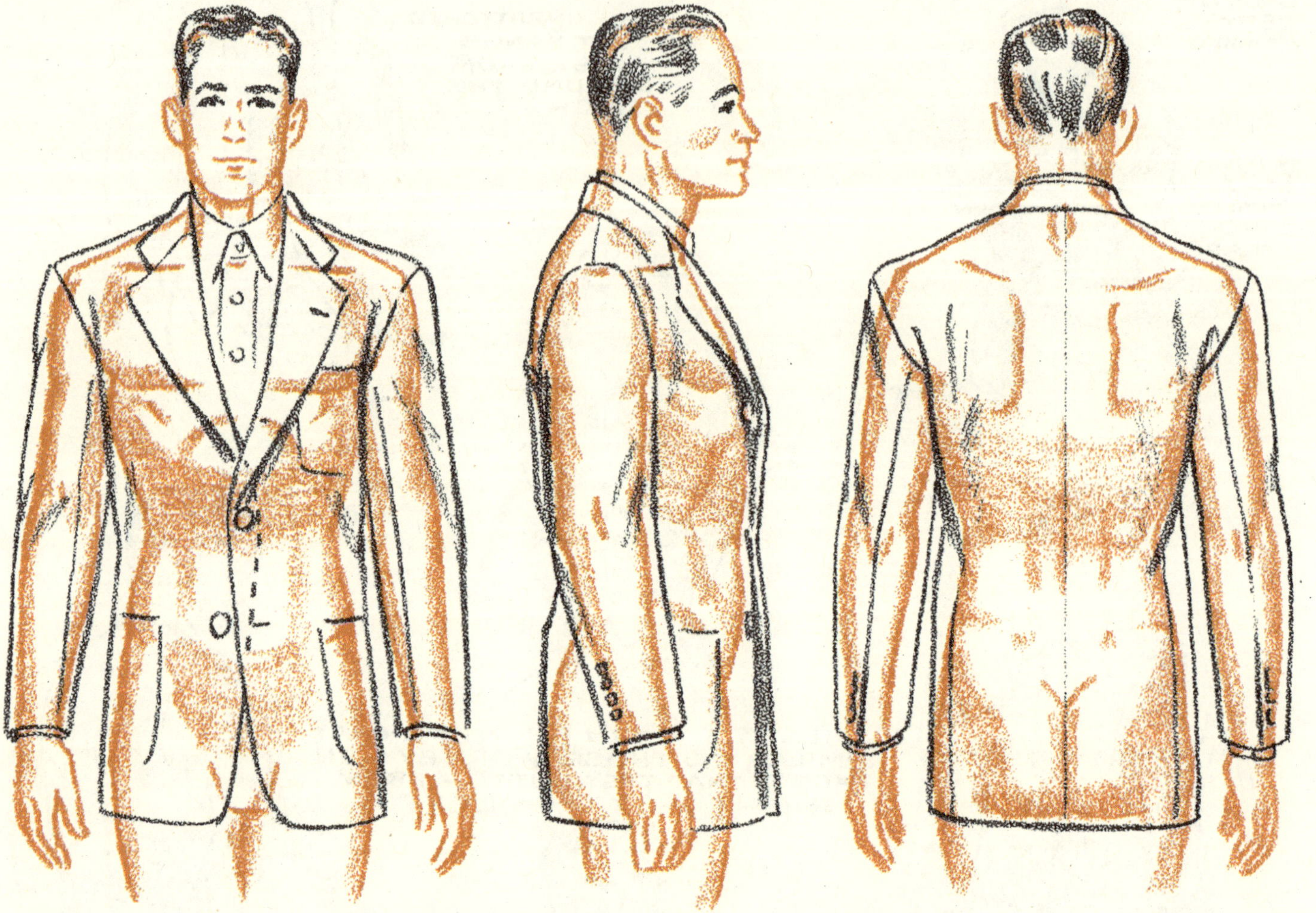

THE JACKET IS WORN OVER THE SHIRT, AND COMES IN ONLY TWO TYPES, SINGLE AND DOUBLE BREASTED. THE LEFT SIDE OF THE JACKET ALWAYS OVERLAPS THE RIGHT IN BUTTONING. THIS IS TRUE OF ALL MEN'S CLOTHING THE OVERCOAT IS WORN OVER ALL OTHER CLOTHES.

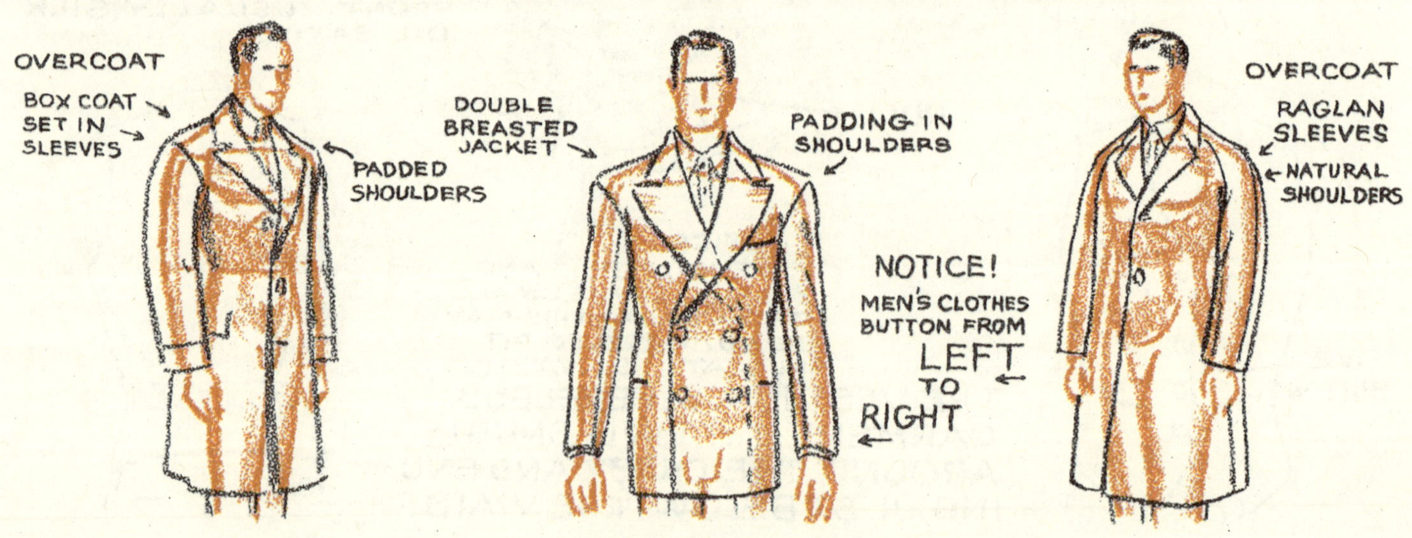

THE JACKET

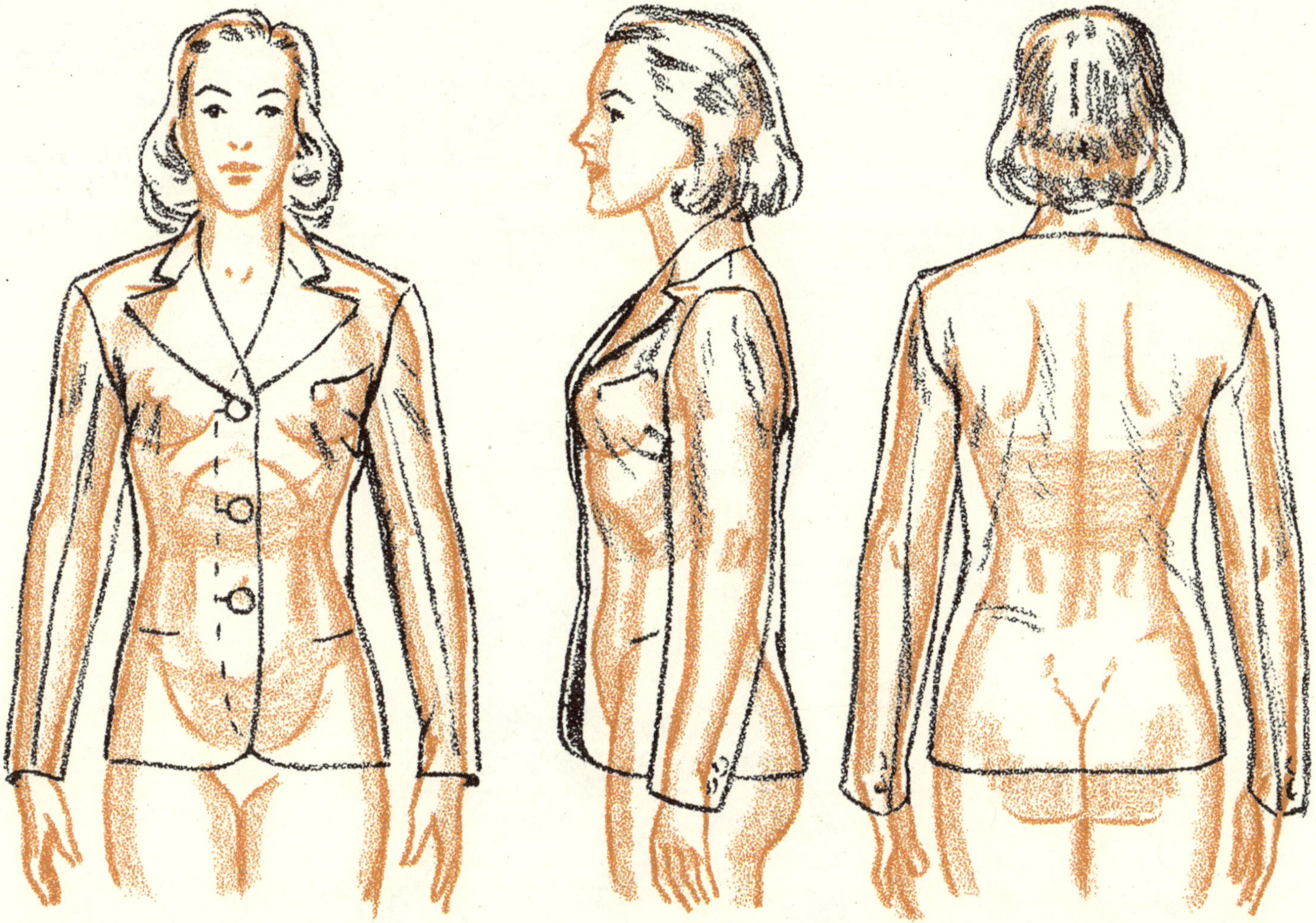

THERE IS MUCH MORE VARIETY IN THE STYLE OF WOMEN'S JACKETS. COLLARS, LAPELS, SLEEVES AND THE LENGTH CHANGE CONSTANTLY. MAKE ANALYSIS DRAWINGS FROM PHOTOS IN FASHION MAGAZINES TO LEARN THE SMART AND NEW STYLES. COMPARE YOUR DRAWINGS WITH THE SIMPLE JACKET SHOWN ABOVE.

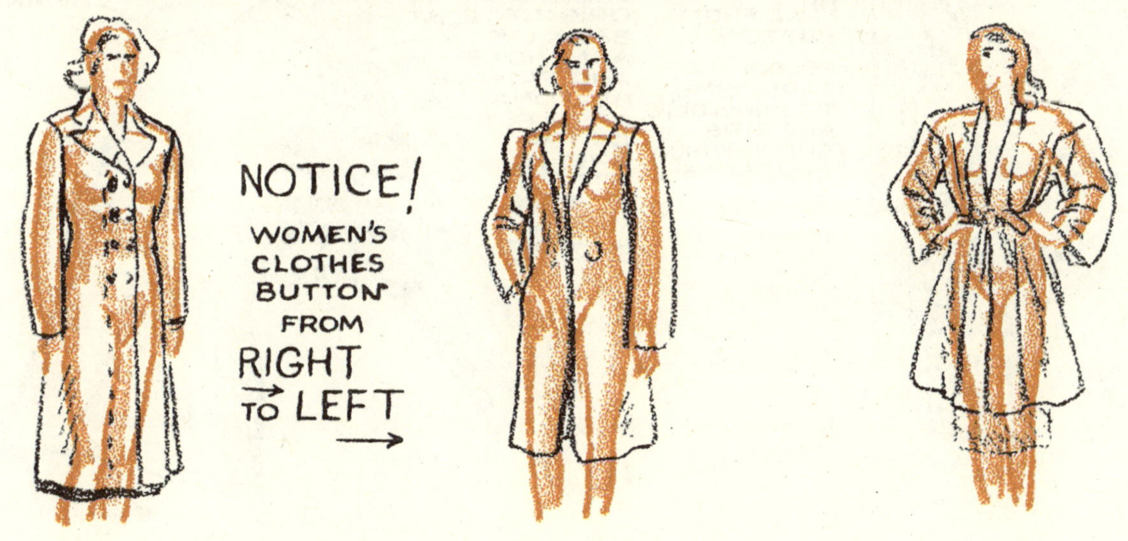

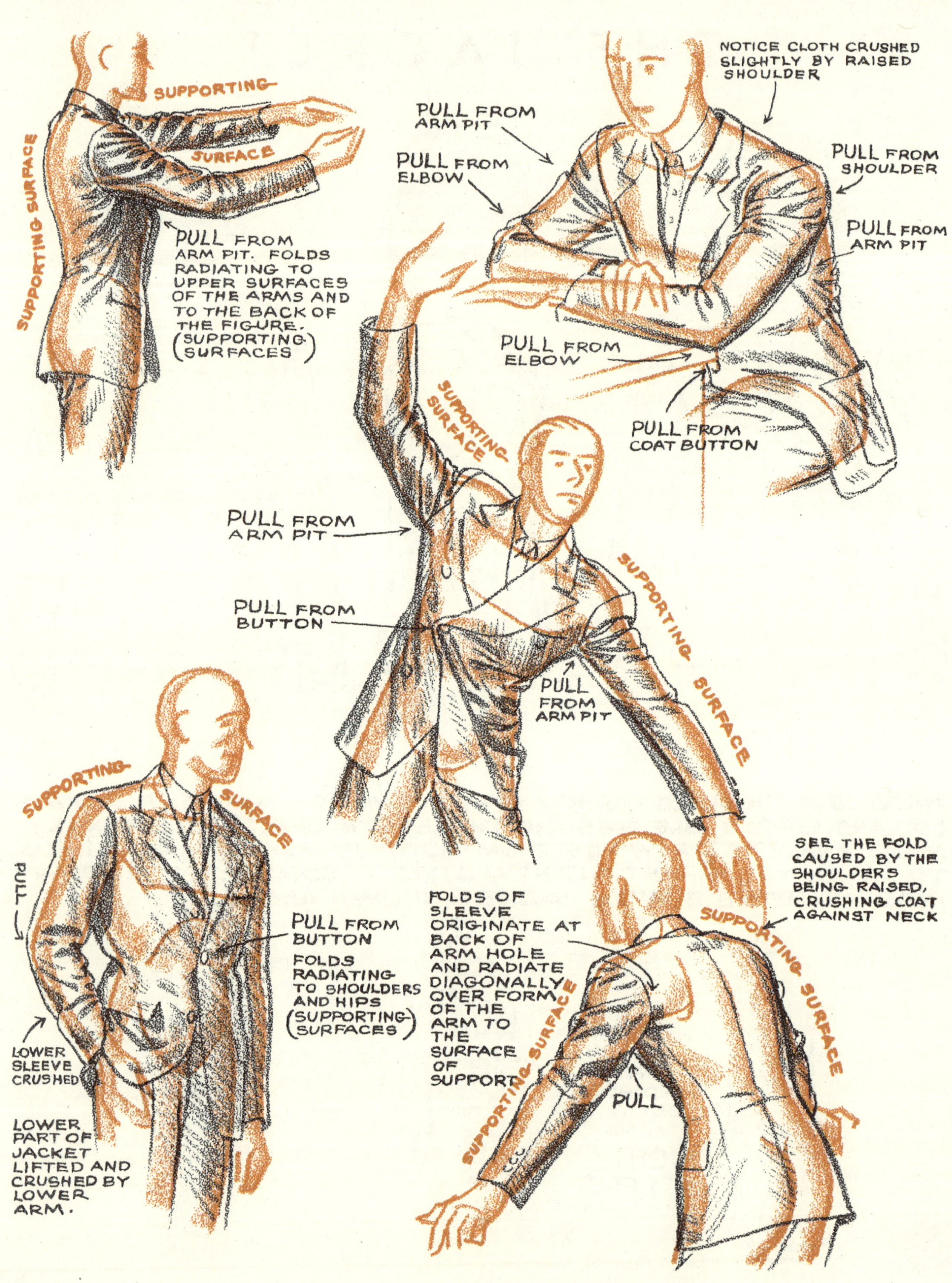
SUPPORTING
SURFACE
SUPPORTING SURFACE
PULL FROM ARM PIT. FOLDS RADIATING TO UPPER SURFACES OF THE ARMS AND TO THE BACK OF THE FIGURE. (SUPPORTING SURFACES)
NOTICE CLOTH CRUSHED SLIGHTLY BY RAISED SHOULDER
PULL FROM ARM PIT
PULL FROM ELBOW
PULL FROM SHOULDER
PULL FROM ARM PIT
PULL FROM ELBOW
PULL FROM COAT BUTTON
SUPPORTING SURFACE
PULL FROM ARM PIT
PULL FROM BUTTON
SUPPORTING SURFACE
PULL FROM ARM PIT
SUPPORTING
SURFACE
PULL
PULL FROM BUTTON
FOLDS RADIATING TO SHOULDERS AND HIPS (SUPPORTING SURFACES)
LOWER SLEEVE CRUSHED
LOWER PART OF JACKET LIFTED AND CRUSHED BY LOWER ARM.
FOLDS OF SLEEVE ORIGINATE AT BACK OF ARM HOLE AND RADIATE DIAGONALLY OVER FORM OF THE ARM TO THE SURFACE OF SUPPORT
SEE THE FOLD CAUSED BY THE SHOULDERS BEING RAISED, CRUSHING COAT AGAINST NECK
SUPPORTING SURFACE
SUPPORTING SURFACE
PULL

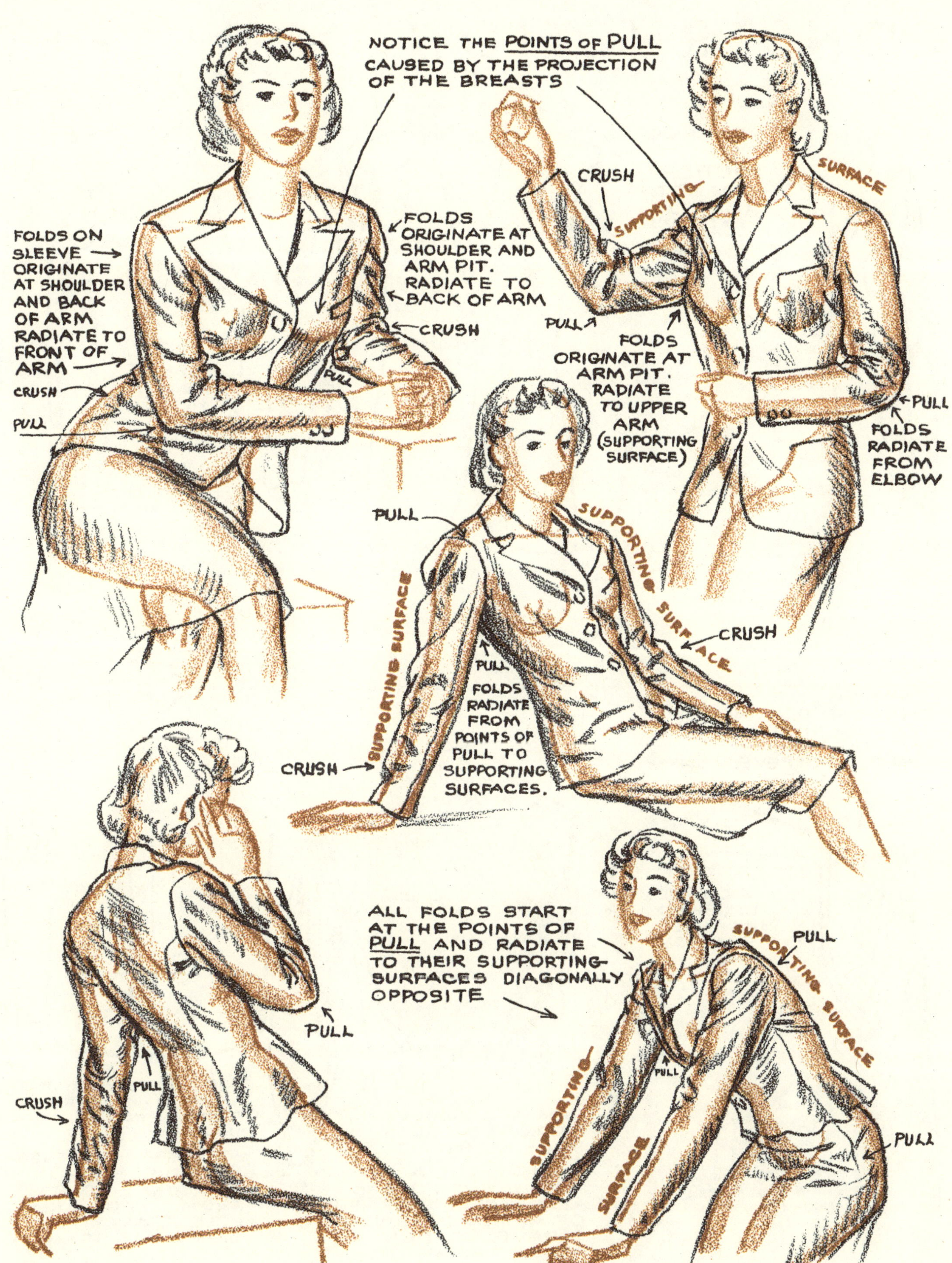
NOTICE THE POINTS OF PULL CAUSED BY THE PROJECTION OF THE BREASTS
FOLDS ON SLEEVE ORIGINATE AT SHOULDER AND BACK OF ARM RADIATE TO FRONT OF ARM
CRUSH
PULL
FOLDS ORIGINATE AT SHOULDER AND ARM PIT. RADIATE TO BACK OF ARM
CRUSH
PULL
CRUSH
SUPPORTING SURFACE
PULL
FOLDS ORIGINATE AT ARM PIT. RADIATE TO UPPER ARM (SUPPORTING SURFACE)
PULL
FOLDS RADIATE FROM ELBOW
PULL
SUPPORTING SURFACE
CRUSH
SUPPORTING SURFACE
PULL
FOLDS RADIATE FROM POINTS OF PULL TO SUPPORTING SURFACES.
CRUSH
ALL FOLDS START AT THE POINTS OF PULL AND RADIATE TO THEIR SUPPORTING SURFACES DIAGONALLY OPPOSITE
PULL
SUPPORTING SURFACE
PULL
PULL
CRUSH
PULL
SUPPORTING SURFACE
PULL

CONSTRUCTION OF JACKET

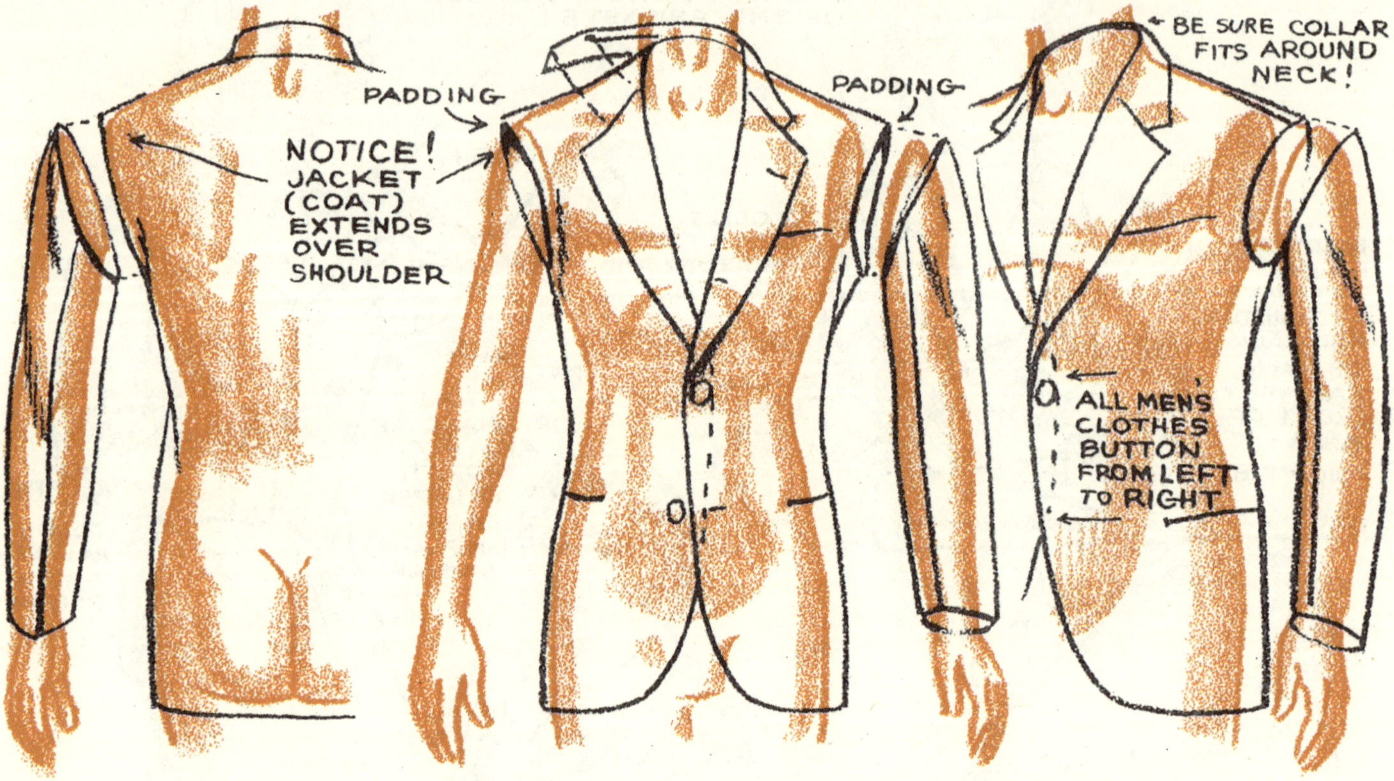

PADDING

NOTICE! JACKET (COAT) EXTENDS OVER SHOULDER

PADDING

BE SURE COLLAR FITS AROUND NECK!

ALL MENS CLOTHES BUTTON FROM LEFT TO RIGHT

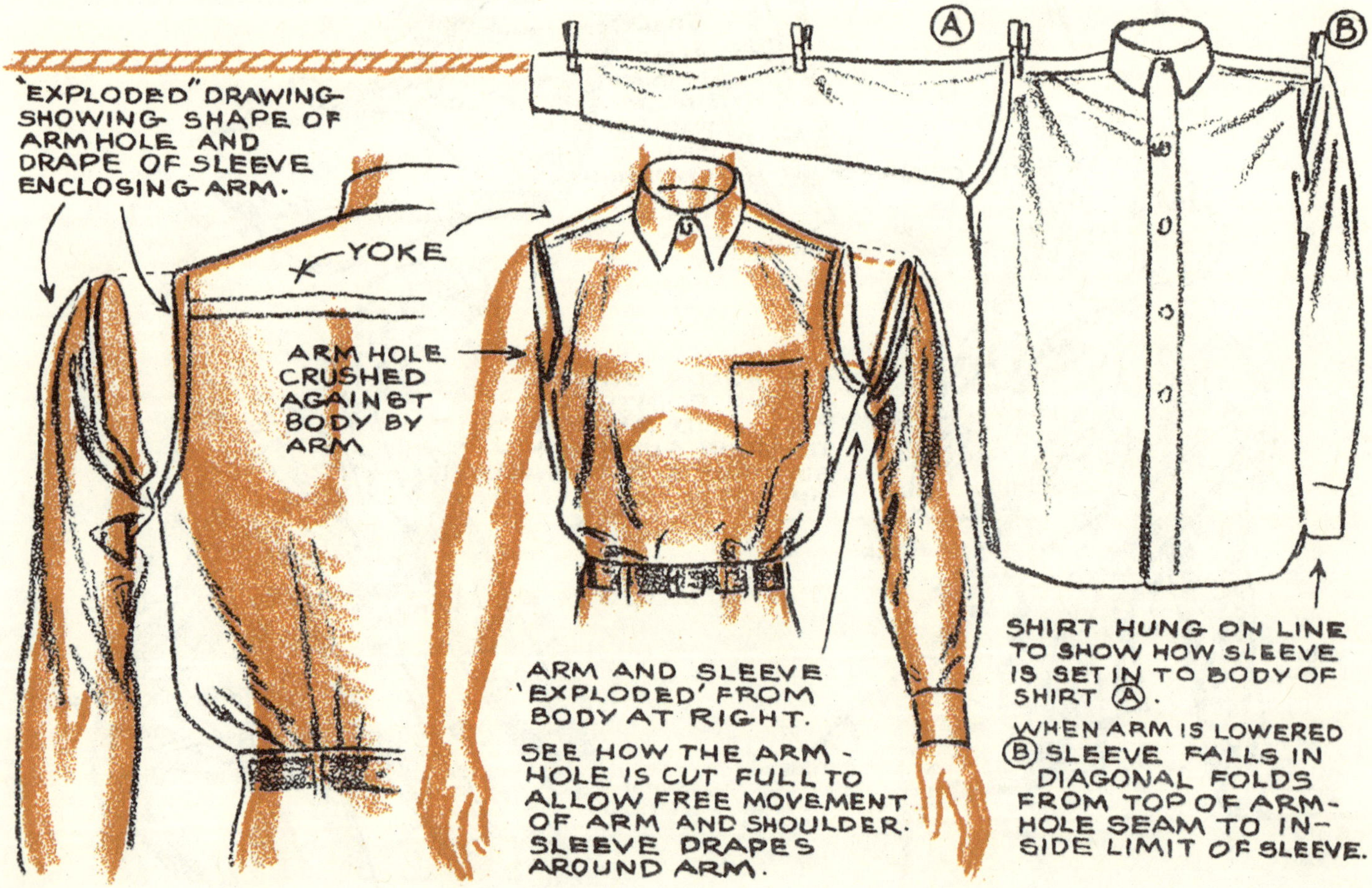

"EXPLODED" DRAWING SHOWING SHAPE OF ARM HOLE AND DRAPE OF SLEEVE ENCLOSING ARM.

YOKE

ARM HOLE CRUSHED AGAINST BODY BY ARM

Ⓐ

Ⓑ

ARM AND SLEEVE 'EXPLODED' FROM BODY AT RIGHT.

SEE HOW THE ARM-HOLE IS CUT FULL TO ALLOW FREE MOVEMENT OF ARM AND SHOULDER. SLEEVE DRAPES AROUND ARM.

SHIRT HUNG ON LINE TO SHOW HOW SLEEVE IS SET IN TO BODY OF SHIRT Ⓐ.

WHEN ARM IS LOWERED Ⓑ SLEEVE FALLS IN DIAGONAL FOLDS FROM TOP OF ARM-HOLE SEAM TO INSIDE LIMIT OF SLEEVE.

DIFFERENCES IN FOLDS-SHIRT-COAT

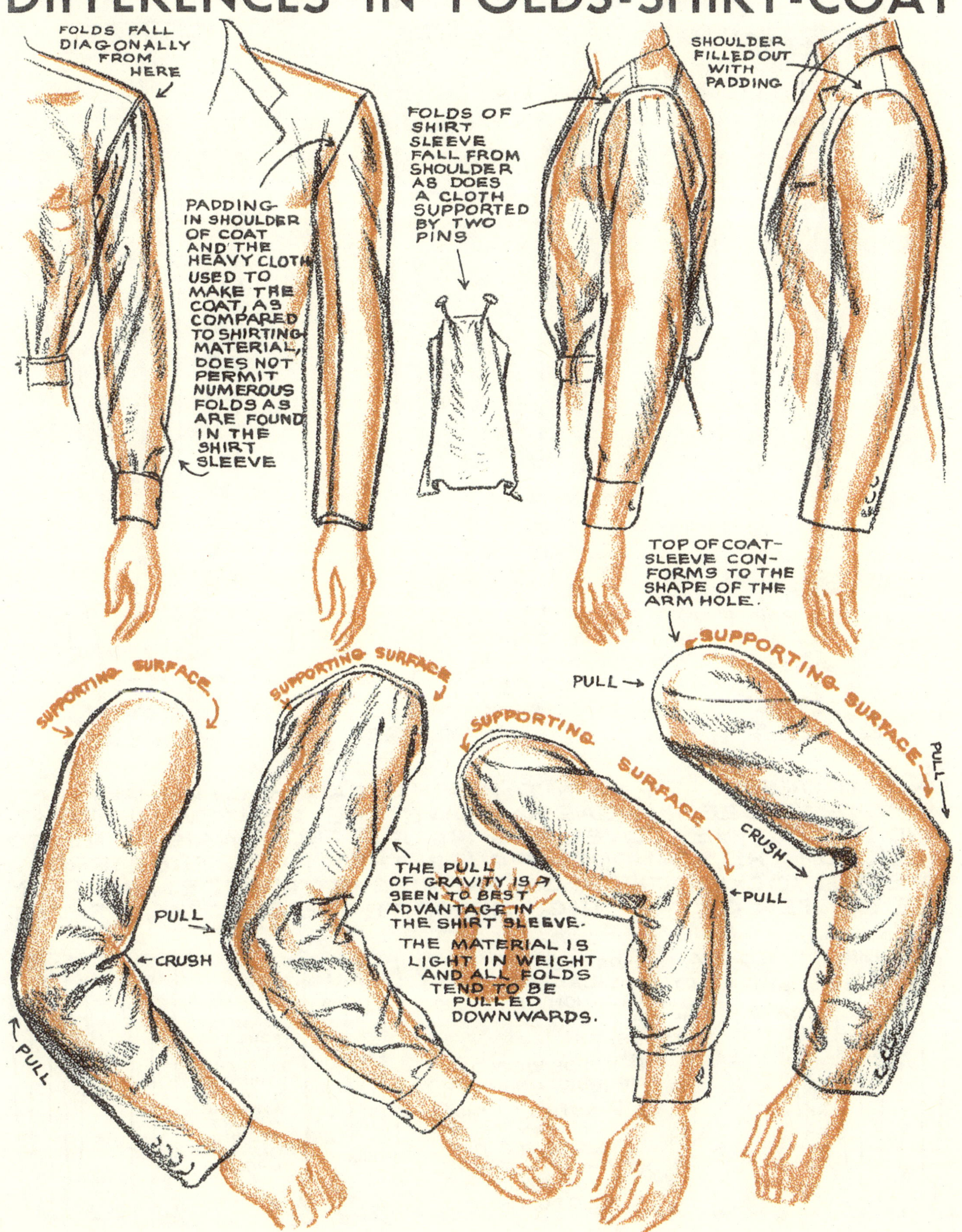

TROUSERS

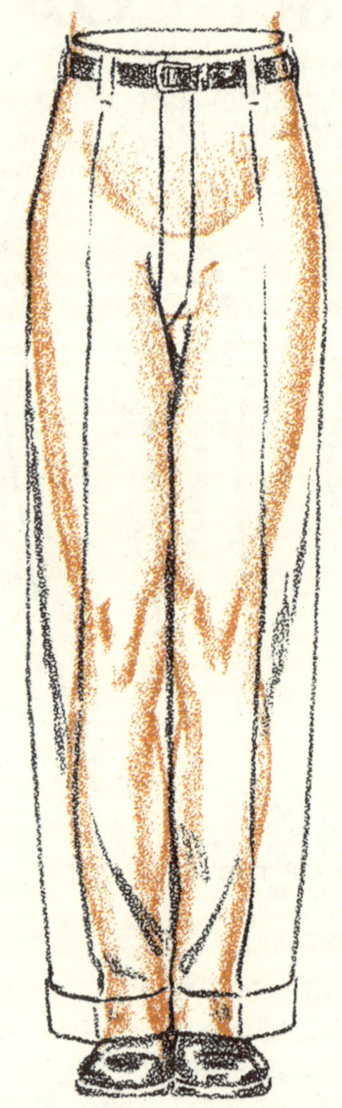

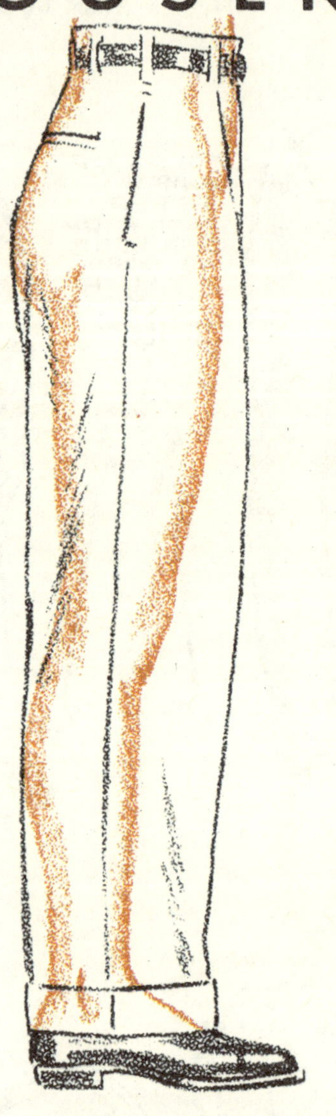

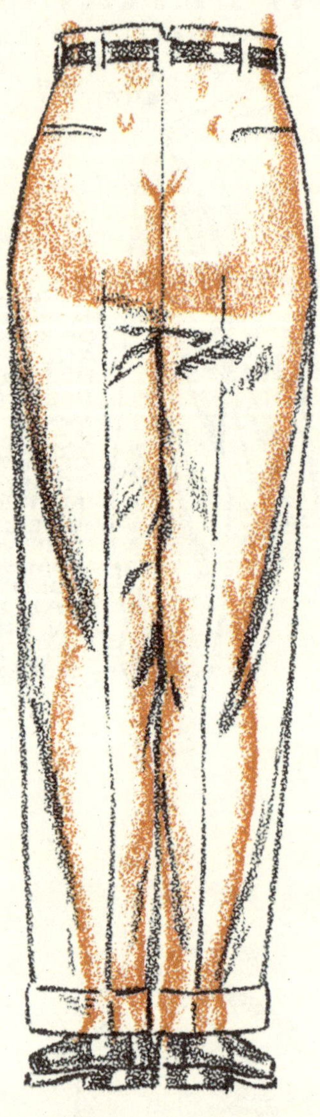

EACH TROUSER LEG IS A TAPERING CLOTH CYLINDER... WHICH HAS BEEN CREASED DOWN THE CENTER IN FRONT AND BACK. THEY COVER THE FIGURE FROM WAIST LINE TO HEEL. ON THE STANDING FIGURE THEY FALL FREE FROM THE BUTTOCKS IN THE BACK, THE HIPS AT THE SIDE, AND FROM THE CENTER OF THE THIGH, OPPOSITE THE BUTTOCKS, IN FRONT.

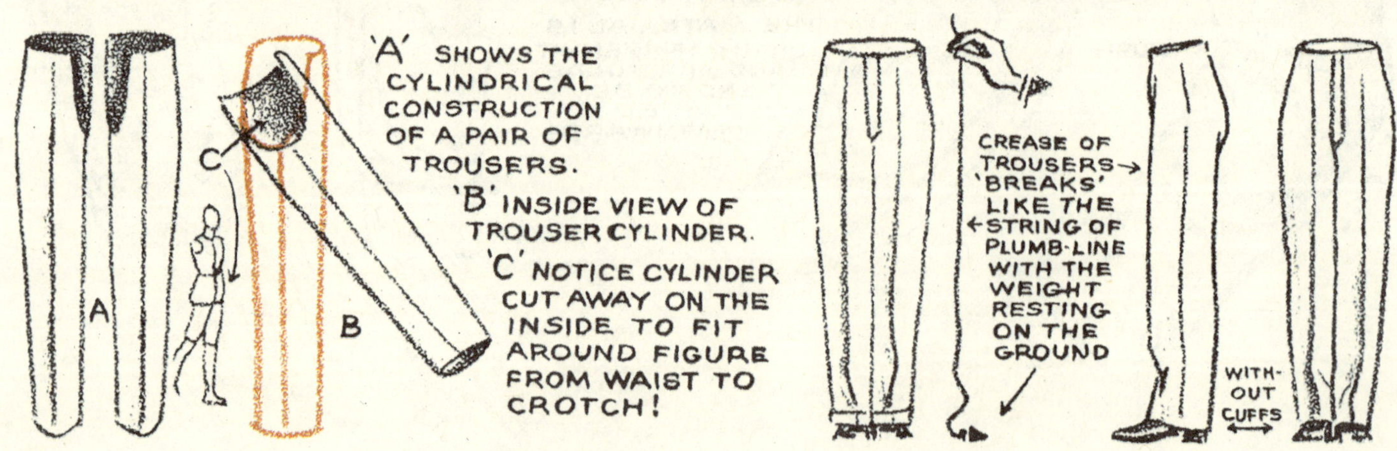

SKIRTS

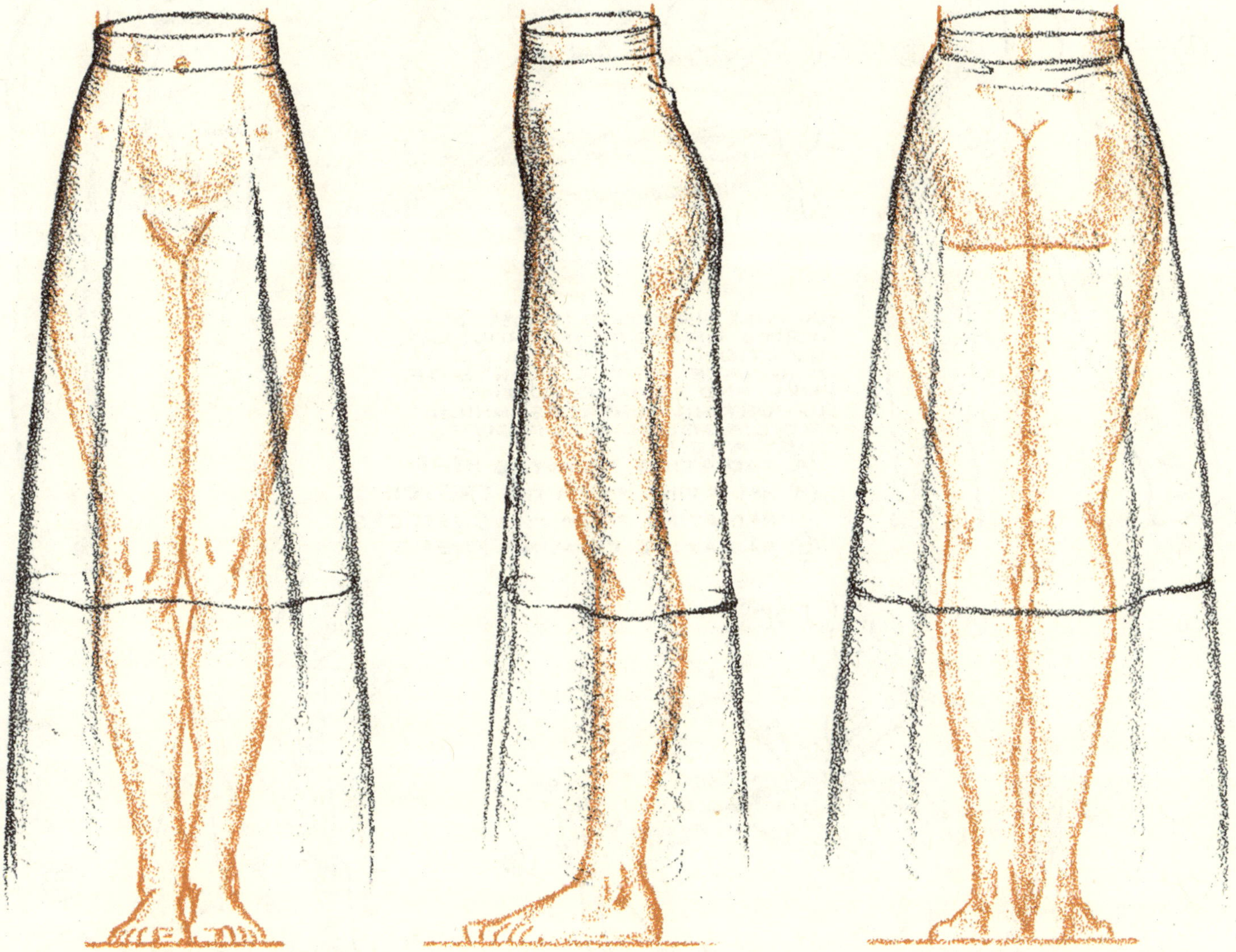

THE SKIRT IS A CONE OF CLOTH THAT FALLS FREE FROM THE FIGURE AT THE BUTTOCKS, HIPS AND THIGHS THE SAME AS TROUSERS. SKIRT STYLES CHANGE FREQUENTLY SO IT IS NECESSARY TO FOLLOW THE FASHION MAGAZINES FOR STYLE TRENDS.

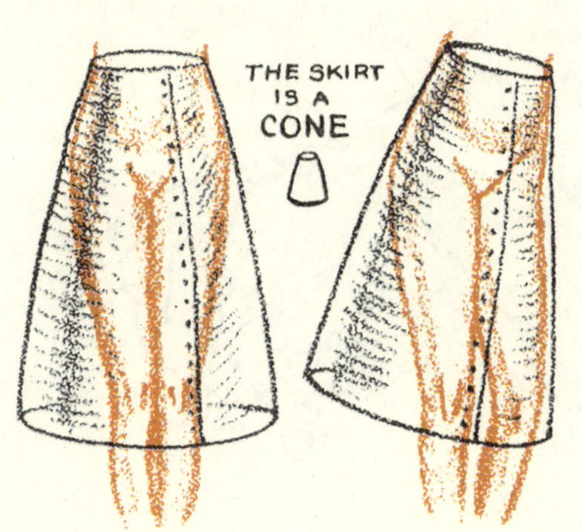

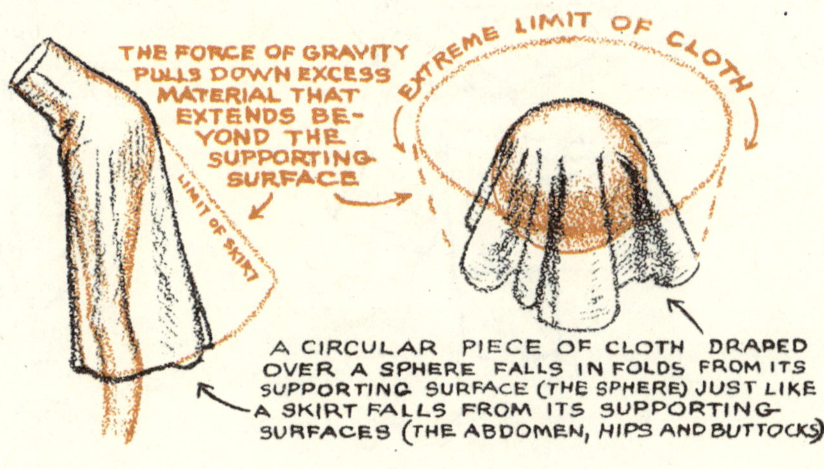

A CIRCULAR PIECE OF CLOTH DRAPED OVER A SPHERE FALLS IN FOLDS FROM ITS SUPPORTING SURFACE (THE SPHERE) JUST LIKE A SKIRT FALLS FROM ITS SUPPORTING SURFACES (THE ABDOMEN, HIPS AND BUTTOCKS)

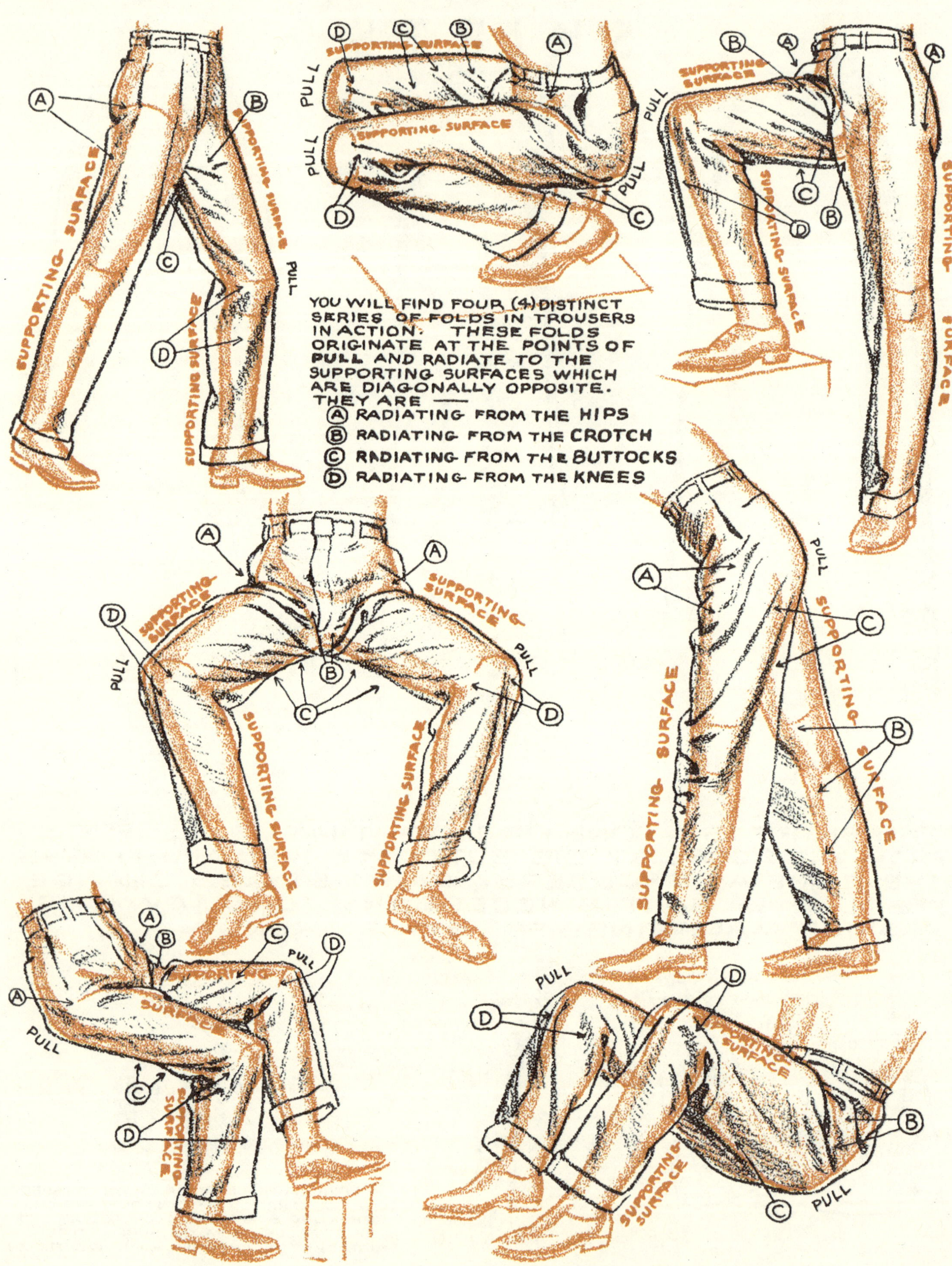
YOU WILL FIND FOUR (4) DISTINCT SERIES OF FOLDS IN TROUSERS IN ACTION. THESE FOLDS ORIGINATE AT THE POINTS OF PULL AND RADIATE TO THE SUPPORTING SURFACES WHICH ARE DIAGONALLY OPPOSITE. THEY ARE —
Ⓐ RADIATING FROM THE HIPS
Ⓑ RADIATING FROM THE CROTCH
Ⓒ RADIATING FROM THE BUTTOCKS
Ⓓ RADIATING FROM THE KNEES
SUPPORTING SURFACE
PULL

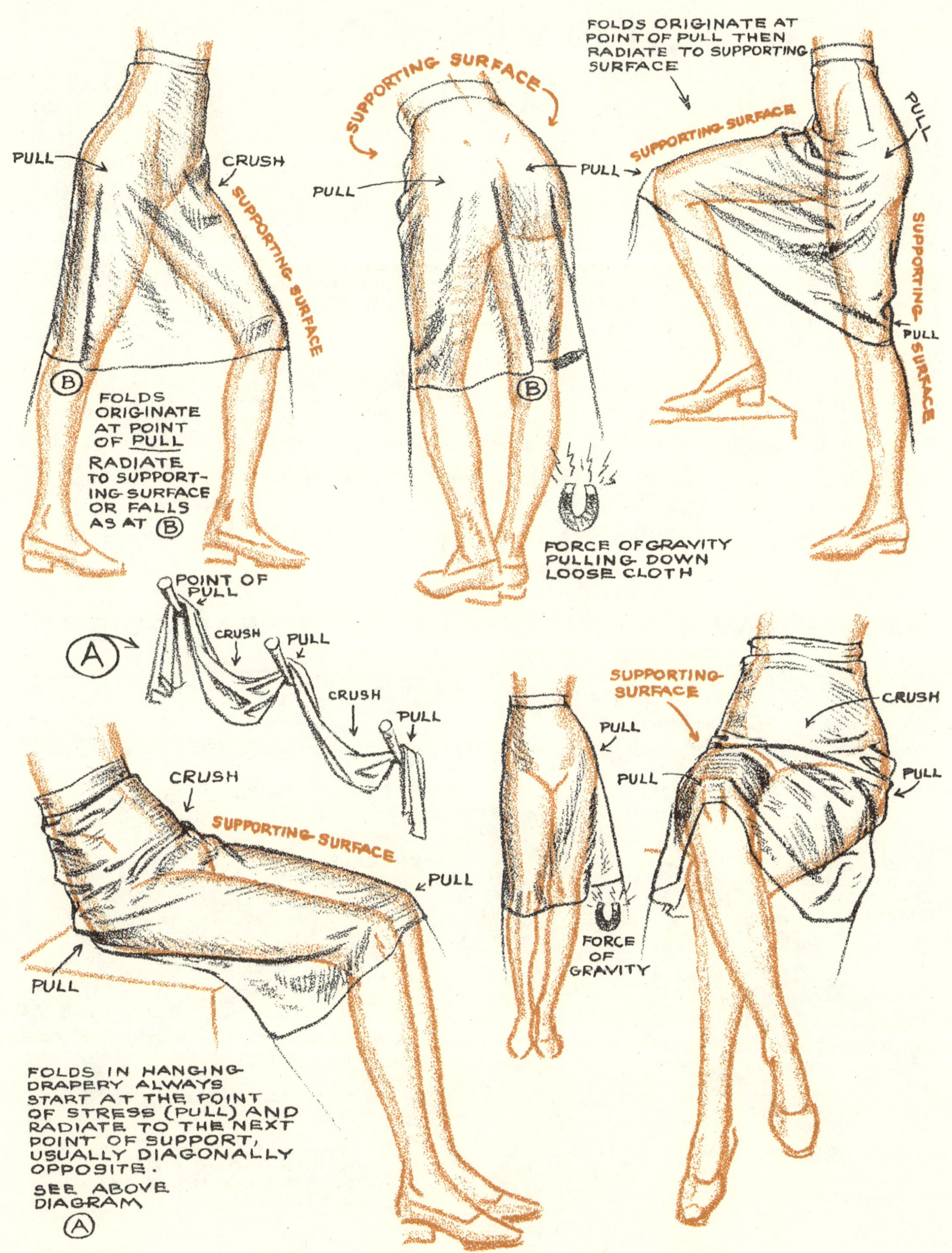
FOLDS ORIGINATE AT POINT OF PULL THEN RADIATE TO SUPPORTING SURFACE
PULL
CRUSH
SUPPORTING SURFACE
FOLDS ORIGINATE AT POINT OF PULL RADIATE TO SUPPORTING SURFACE OR FALLS AS AT (B)
(B)
SUPPORTING SURFACE
PULL
PULL
(B)
FORCE OF GRAVITY PULLING DOWN LOOSE CLOTH
SUPPORTING SURFACE
PULL
PULL
SUPPORTING SURFACE
PULL
POINT OF PULL
(A)
CRUSH
PULL
CRUSH
PULL
CRUSH
SUPPORTING SURFACE
PULL
PULL
PULL
FORCE OF GRAVITY
SUPPORTING SURFACE
CRUSH
PULL
PULL
FOLDS IN HANGING DRAPERY ALWAYS START AT THE POINT OF STRESS (PULL) AND RADIATE TO THE NEXT POINT OF SUPPORT, USUALLY DIAGONALLY OPPOSITE.
SEE ABOVE DIAGRAM (A)

GLOVES FOR MEN

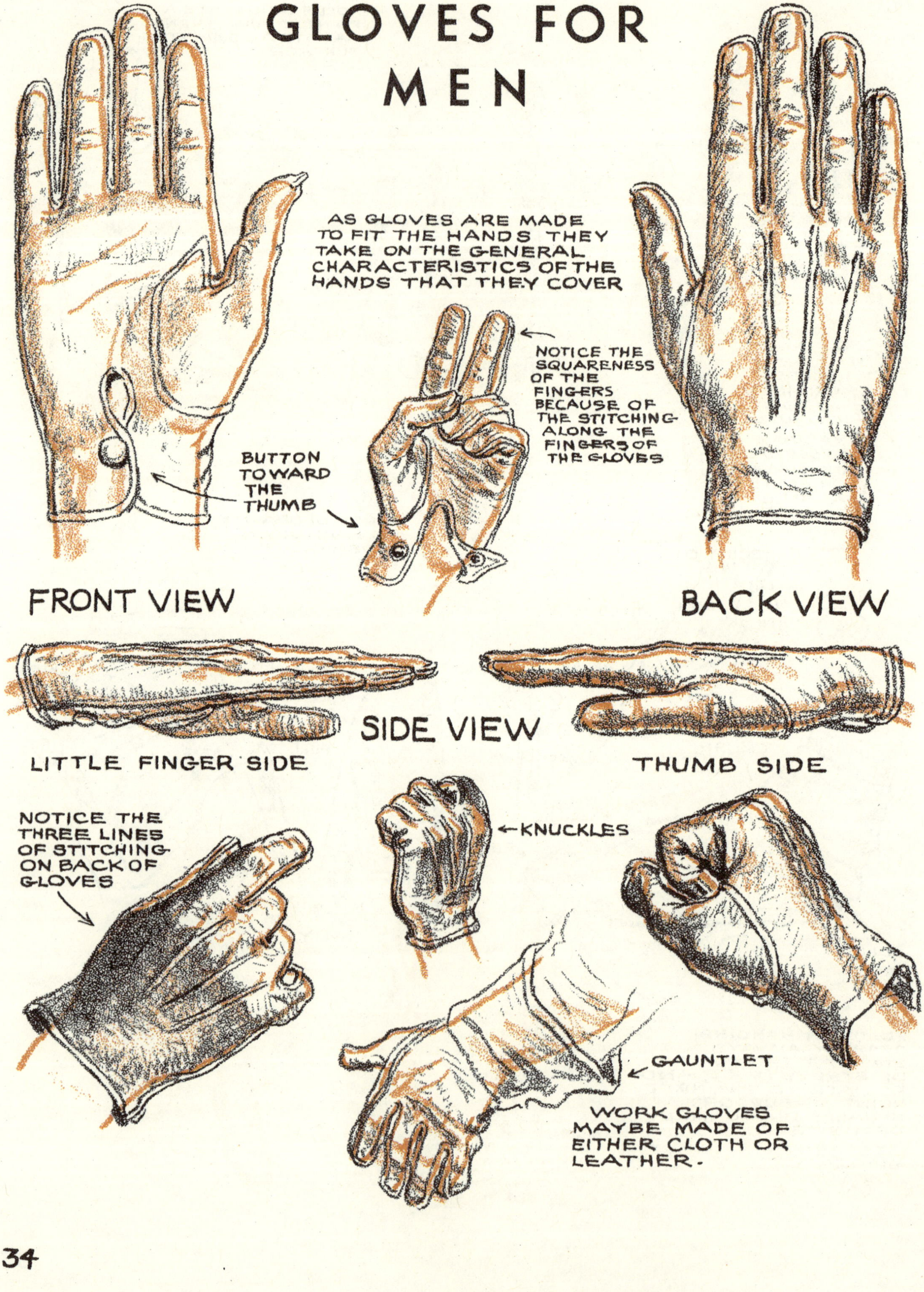

AS GLOVES ARE MADE TO FIT THE HANDS THEY TAKE ON THE GENERAL CHARACTERISTICS OF THE HANDS THAT THEY COVER

NOTICE THE SQUARENESS OF THE FINGERS BECAUSE OF THE STITCHING ALONG THE FINGERS OF THE GLOVES

BUTTON TOWARD THE THUMB

FRONT VIEW

BACK VIEW

SIDE VIEW

LITTLE FINGER SIDE

THUMB SIDE

NOTICE THE THREE LINES OF STITCHING ON BACK OF GLOVES

←KNUCKLES

GAUNTLET

WORK GLOVES MAYBE MADE OF EITHER CLOTH OR LEATHER.

GLOVES FOR WOMEN

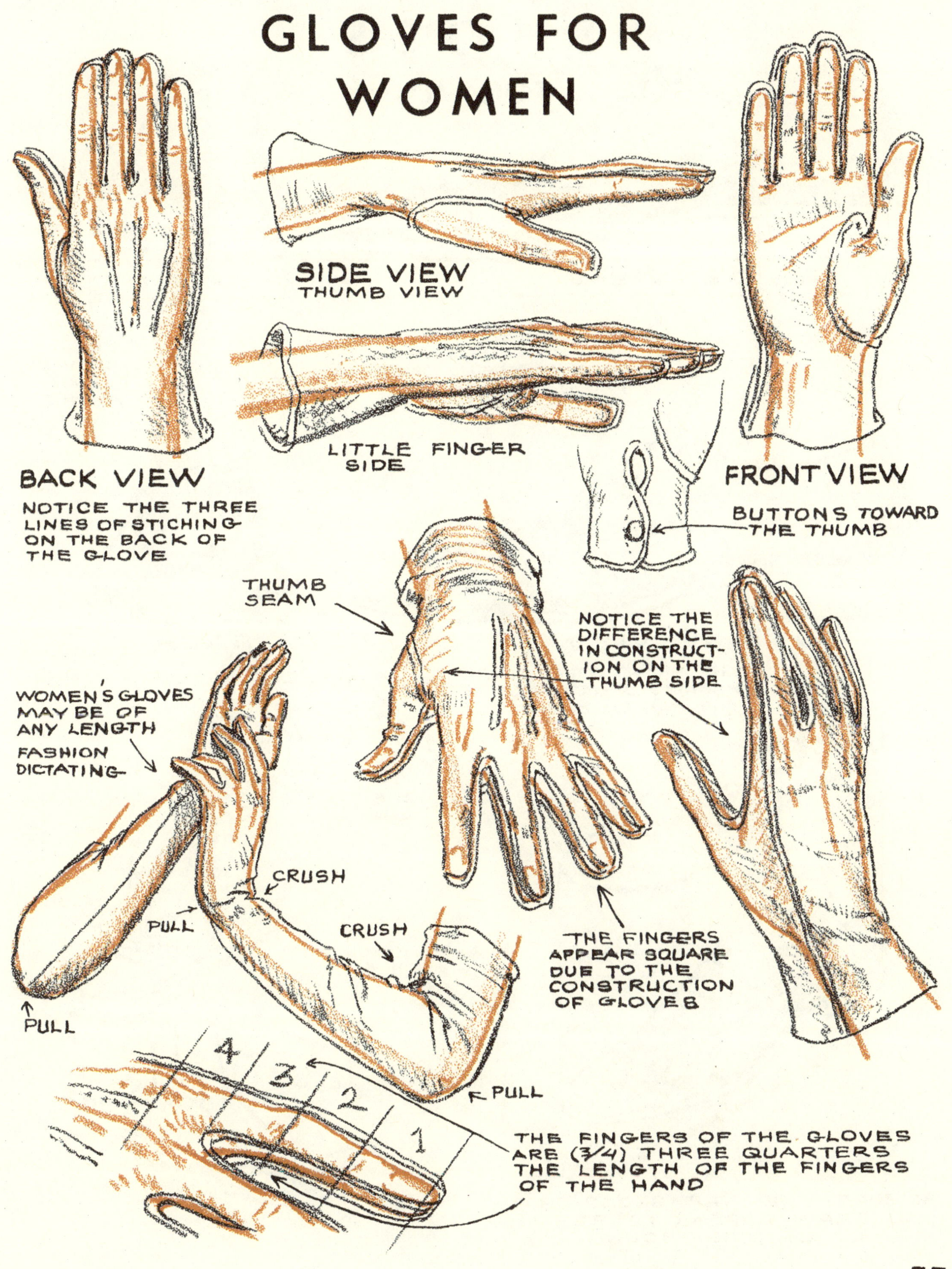

SHOES
FOR MEN

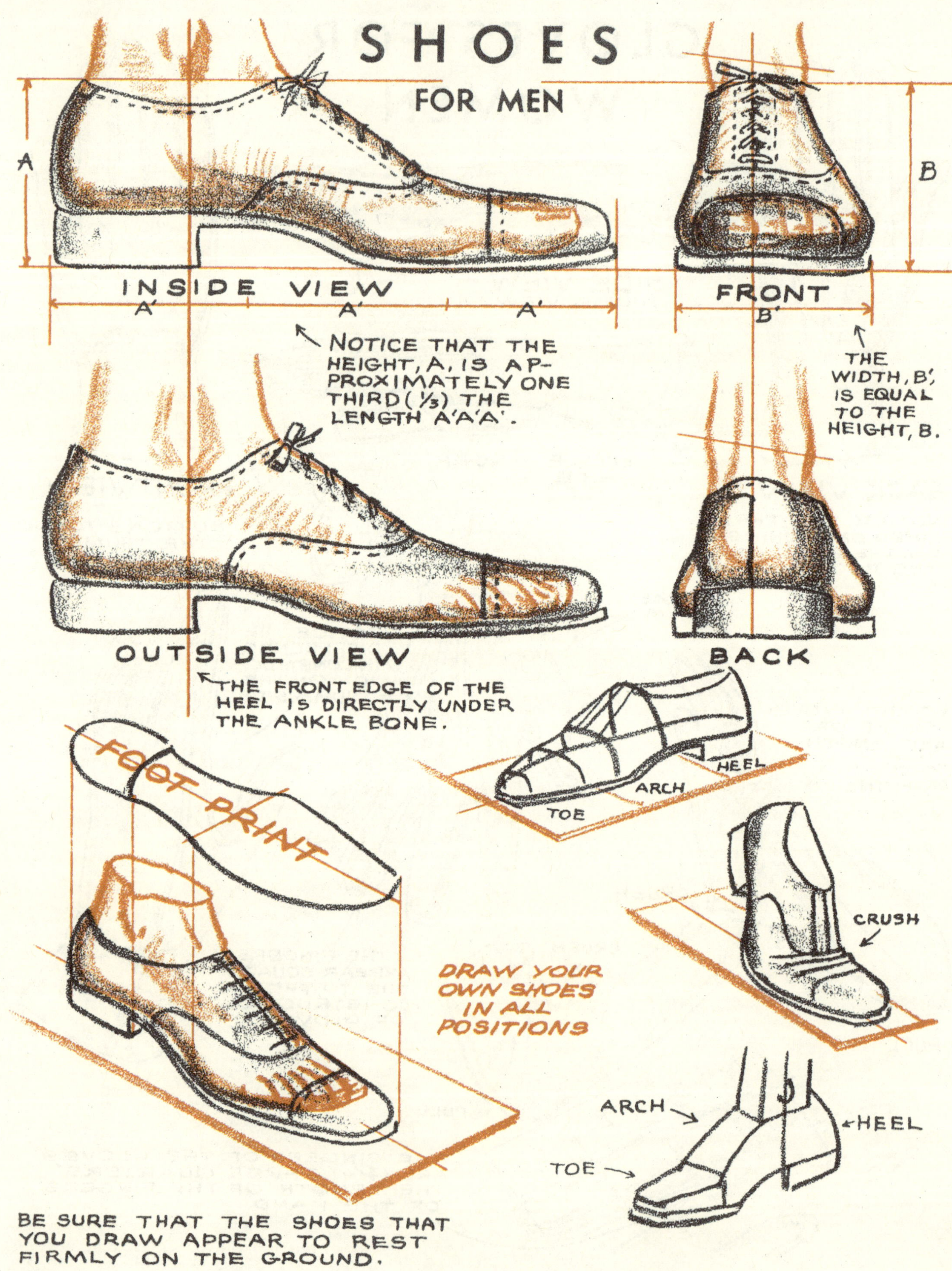

BE SURE THAT THE SHOES THAT YOU DRAW APPEAR TO REST FIRMLY ON THE GROUND.

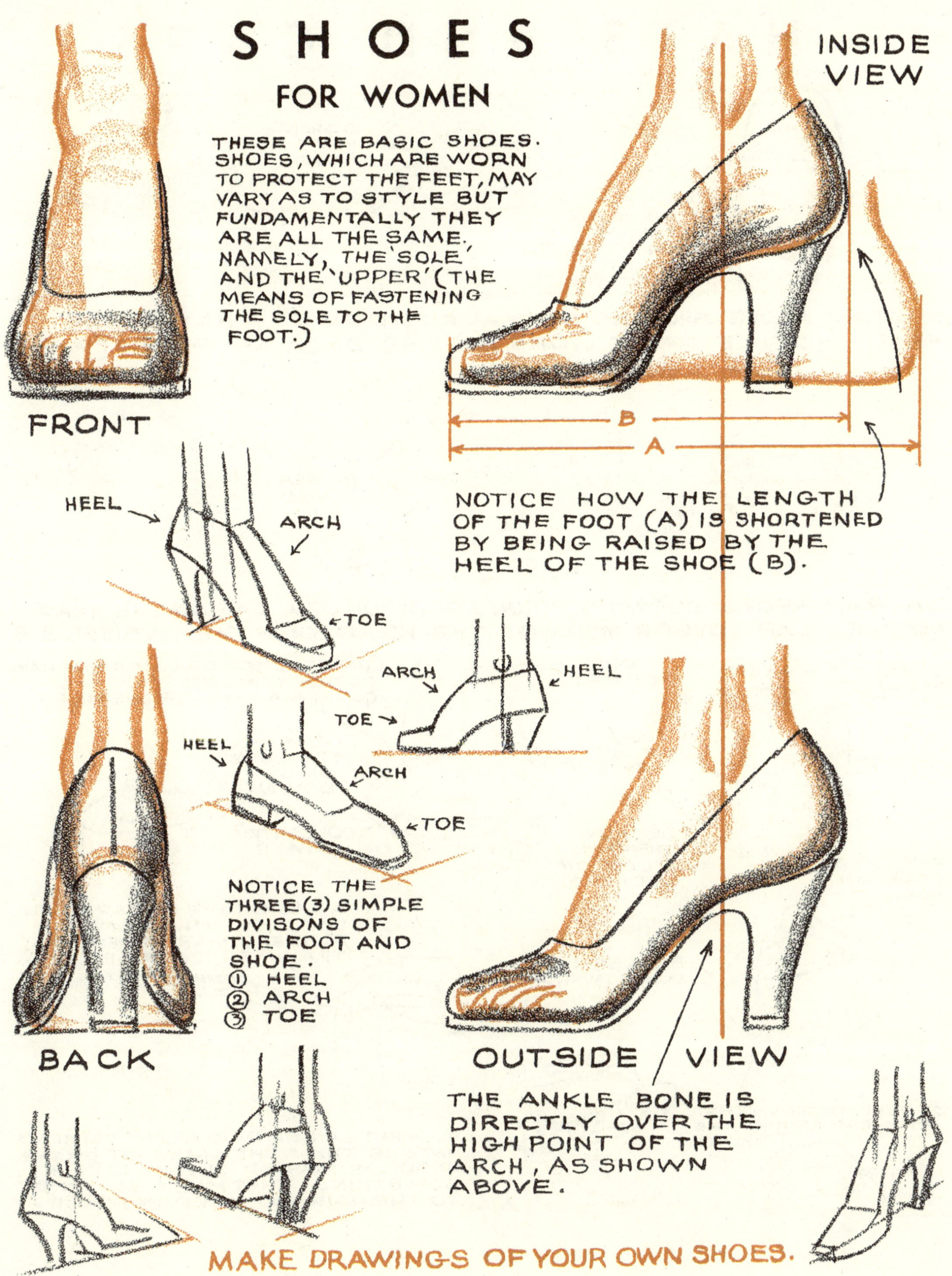
SHOES
FOR WOMEN
THESE ARE BASIC SHOES. SHOES, WHICH ARE WORN TO PROTECT THE FEET, MAY VARY AS TO STYLE BUT FUNDAMENTALLY THEY ARE ALL THE SAME. NAMELY, THE 'SOLE' AND THE 'UPPER' (THE MEANS OF FASTENING THE SOLE TO THE FOOT.)
INSIDE VIEW
FRONT
B
A
NOTICE HOW THE LENGTH OF THE FOOT (A) IS SHORTENED BY BEING RAISED BY THE HEEL OF THE SHOE (B).
HEEL
ARCH
TOE
ARCH
HEEL
TOE
HEEL
ARCH
TOE
NOTICE THE THREE (3) SIMPLE DIVISONS OF THE FOOT AND SHOE.
① HEEL
② ARCH
③ TOE
BACK
OUTSIDE VIEW
THE ANKLE BONE IS DIRECTLY OVER THE HIGH POINT OF THE ARCH, AS SHOWN ABOVE.
MAKE DRAWINGS OF YOUR OWN SHOES.

HATS AND CAPS

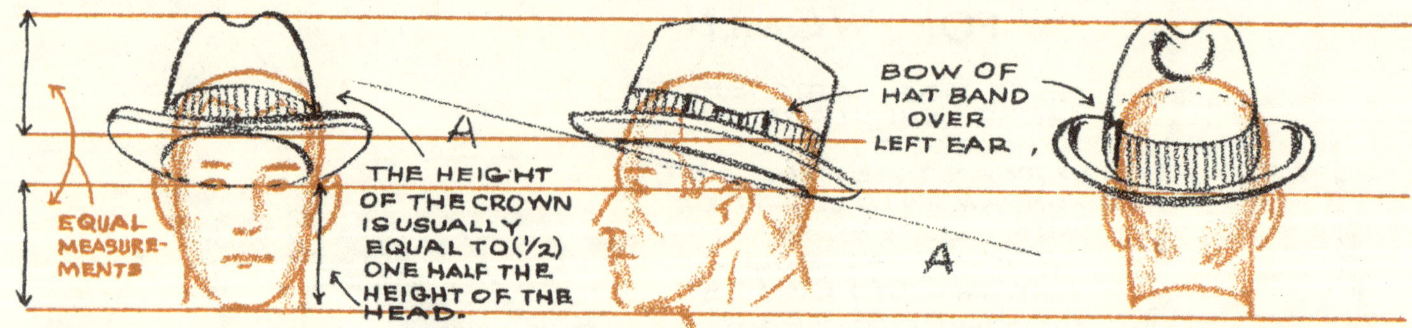

DIAGRAM ABOVE SHOWING NORMAL POSITION OF A HAT ON THE HEAD. NOTICE HAT IS WORN SLOPING BACK AS SHOWN (A–A)

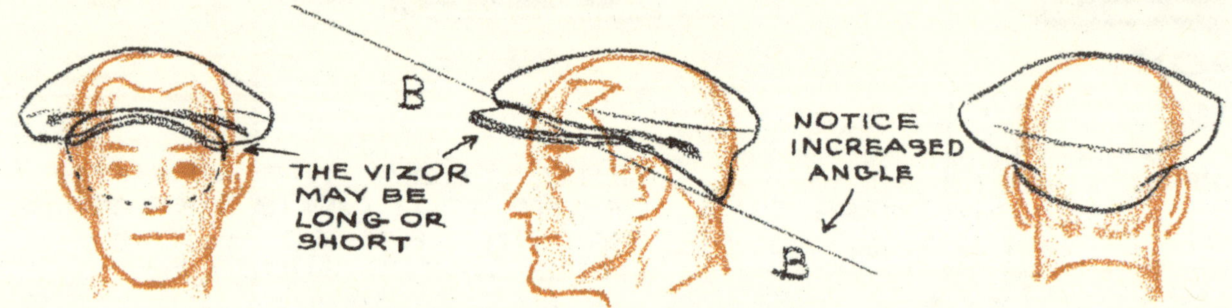

DIAGRAM ABOVE SHOWING NORMAL POSITION OF A CAP ON THE HEAD. NOTICE CAP COVERS MORE OF THE HEAD THAN THE HAT. (SEE B–B)

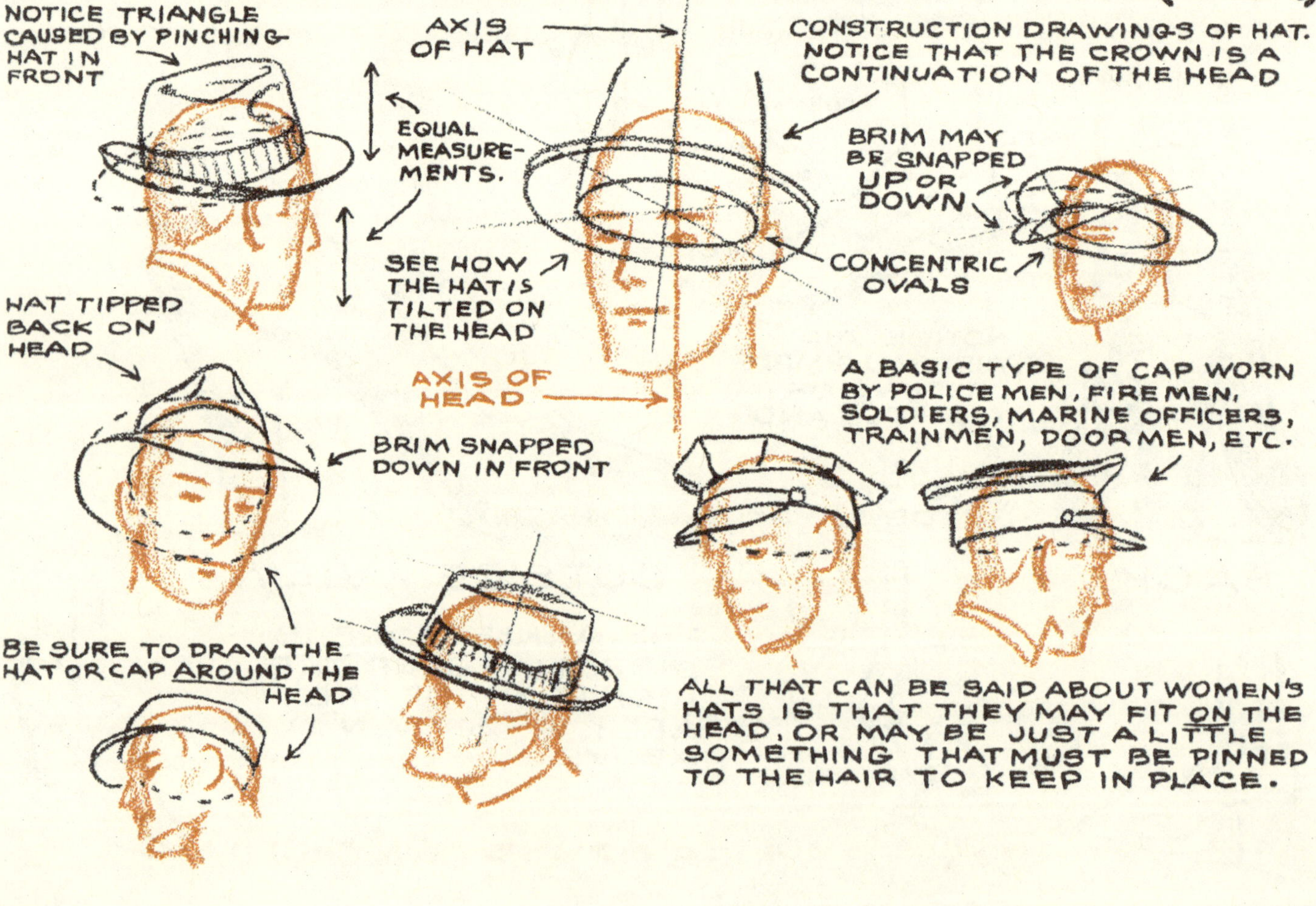

NOTICE TRIANGLE CAUSED BY PINCHING HAT IN FRONT

AXIS OF HAT

CONSTRUCTION DRAWINGS OF HAT. NOTICE THAT THE CROWN IS A CONTINUATION OF THE HEAD

EQUAL MEASURE-MENTS.

BRIM MAY BE SNAPPED UP OR DOWN

SEE HOW THE HAT IS TILTED ON THE HEAD

CONCENTRIC OVALS

HAT TIPPED BACK ON HEAD

AXIS OF HEAD

A BASIC TYPE OF CAP WORN BY POLICE MEN, FIRE MEN, SOLDIERS, MARINE OFFICERS, TRAINMEN, DOOR MEN, ETC.

BRIM SNAPPED DOWN IN FRONT

BE SURE TO DRAW THE HAT OR CAP AROUND THE HEAD

ALL THAT CAN BE SAID ABOUT WOMEN'S HATS IS THAT THEY MAY FIT ON THE HEAD, OR MAY BE JUST A LITTLE SOMETHING THAT MUST BE PINNED TO THE HAIR TO KEEP IN PLACE.

MAKING USE OF PHOTOGRAPHS TO STUDY DRAPERY OF CLOTHES

The thousands of photos found in newspapers and magazines are all for your use to assist you in your study of drapery.

The plan which I followed is—

STEP ONE:—Tear a photograph of a clothed figure out of a magazine or newspaper.

STEP TWO:—Make a simple but accurate drawing of the figure with a colored pencil. It is advisable to keep this drawing in simple solids, making sure that the cylindrical forms are shown in their correct relation in space—that is, to show that they are coming forward or going back, raised or lowered, as may be indicated by your photograph.

STEP THREE:—Then, with black pencil, draw in the clothes, paying particular attention to the direction of the folds caused by action of the figure.

Since these drawings are made to increase your knowledge of clothing and drapery—do them as accurately as possible.

Remember, you are not trying to improve or correct the photograph—you are simply making studies to gather more and more knowledge of drapery and the appearance of clothing on figures in action. You always go to nature (either drawing direct from the model or from photos) for knowledge and you then study the work of artists to understand how knowledge may be designed, or in other words—used most effectively. It might be helpful to analyze the clothed figures in magazine illustrations to see how the artist used the knowledge of drapery in designing the folds of the clothes to make the action of the figure attractive and easy to understand.

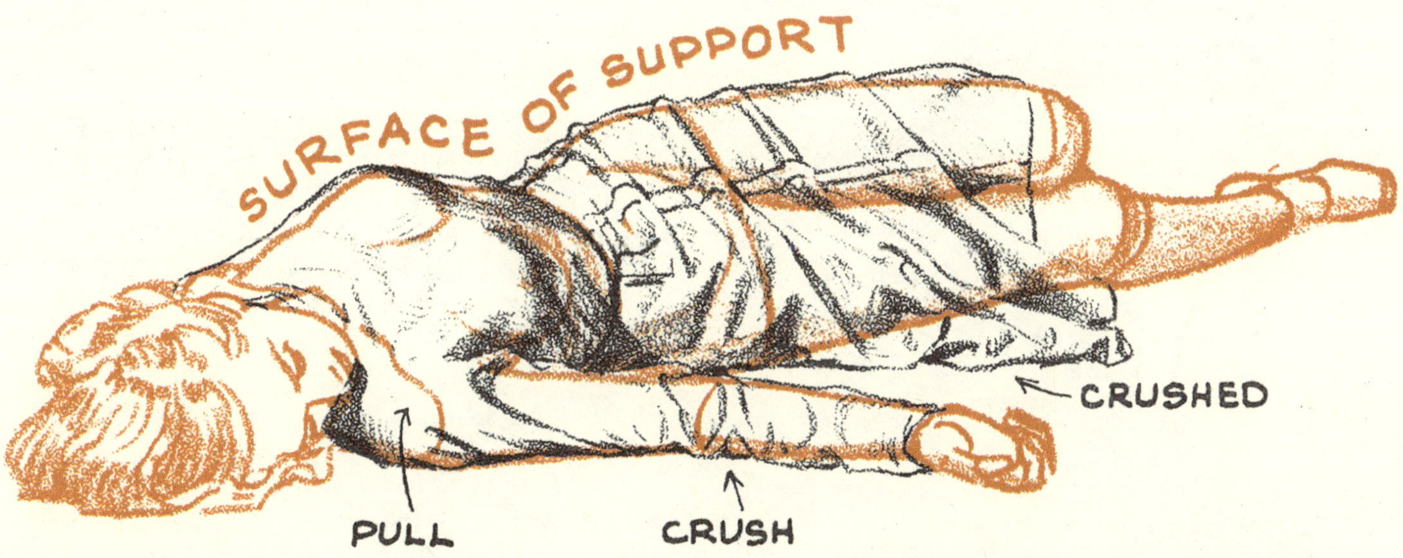

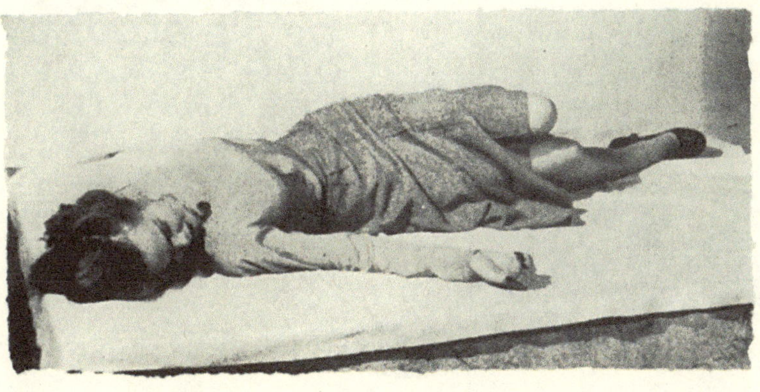

NOTICE THE FOLDS OF THE SKIRT FALLING OVER THE UPPER LEG (PRIMARY SURFACE OF SUPPORT) TO THE LOWER LEG (SECONDARY SURFACE OF SUPPORT) AND FROM THERE TO THE FLOOR.

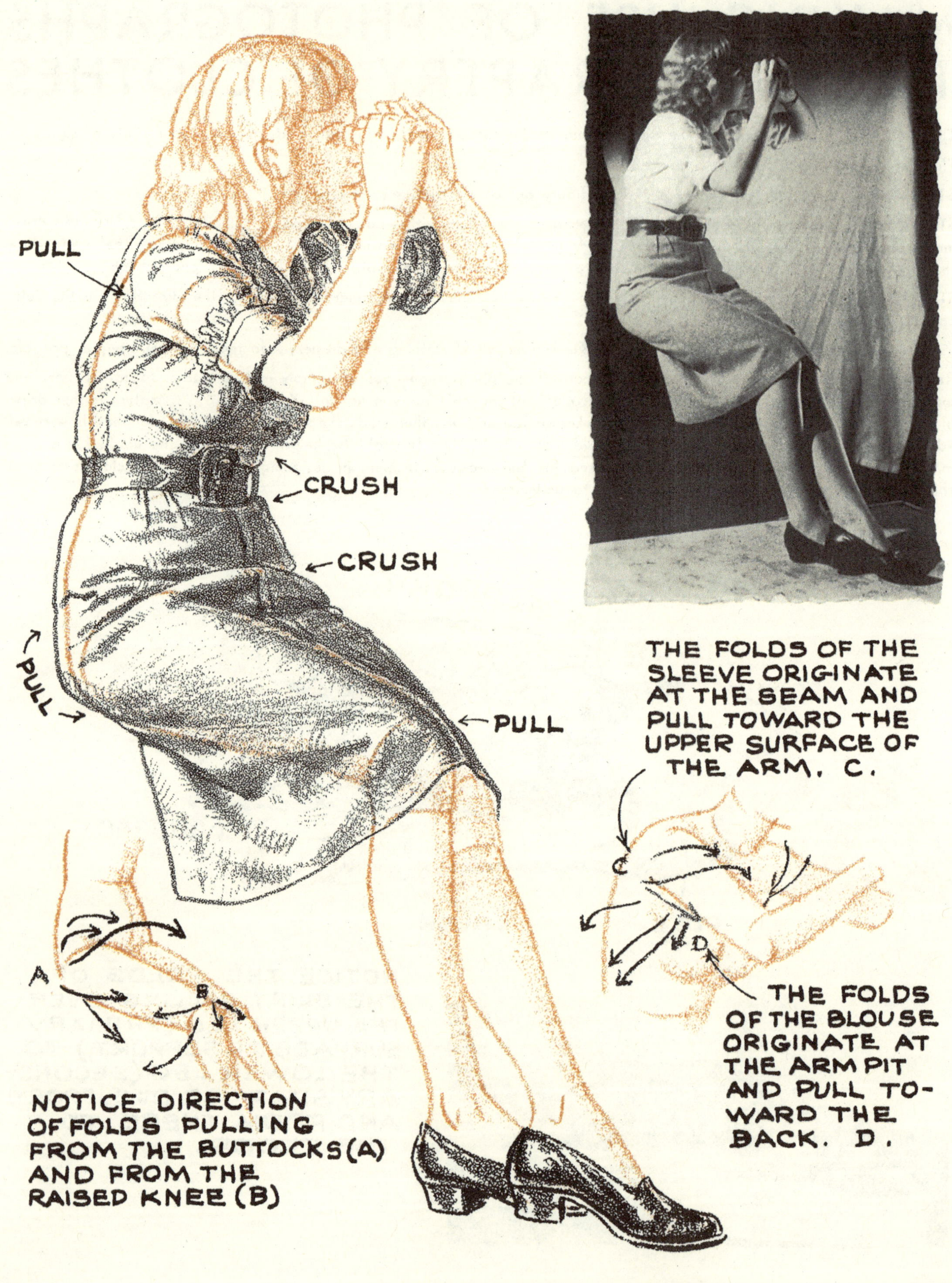
PULL
CRUSH
CRUSH
PULL
PULL
A
B
C
D
THE FOLDS OF THE SLEEVE ORIGINATE AT THE SEAM AND PULL TOWARD THE UPPER SURFACE OF THE ARM. C.
THE FOLDS OF THE BLOUSE ORIGINATE AT THE ARM PIT AND PULL TO-WARD THE BACK. D.
NOTICE DIRECTION OF FOLDS PULLING FROM THE BUTTOCKS (A) AND FROM THE RAISED KNEE (B)

THE PHOTO, SHOWN BELOW, WAS THE MODEL FROM WHICH THIS DRAWING WAS MADE.
MAKE DRAWINGS FROM PHOTOS THAT YOU WILL FIND EVERY DAY IN NEWS PAPERS AND MAGAZINES.

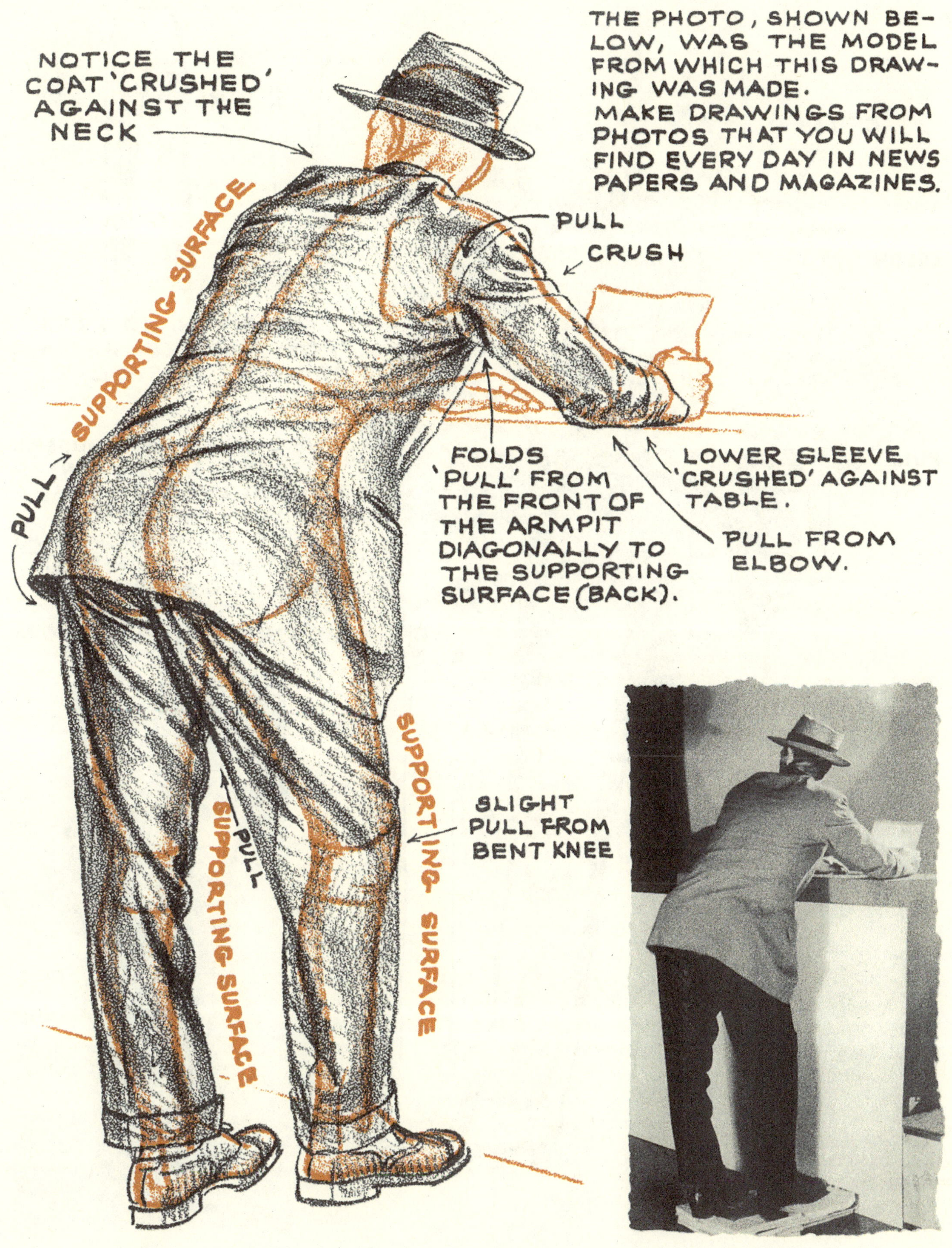

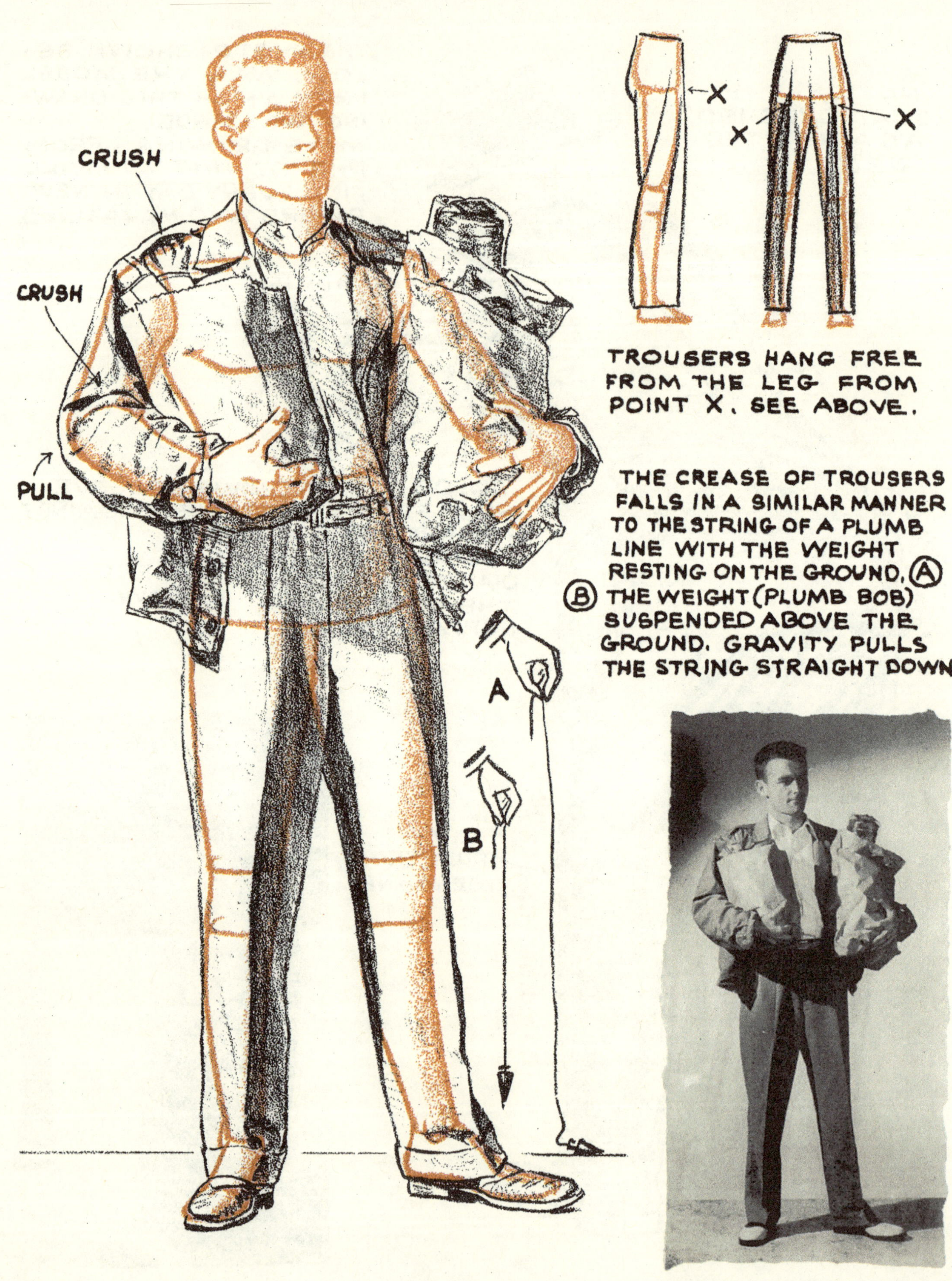
CRUSH
CRUSH
PULL
X
X
X
TROUSERS HANG FREE FROM THE LEG FROM POINT X. SEE ABOVE.
THE CREASE OF TROUSERS FALLS IN A SIMILAR MANNER TO THE STRING OF A PLUMB LINE WITH THE WEIGHT RESTING ON THE GROUND, (A) (B) THE WEIGHT (PLUMB BOB) SUSPENDED ABOVE THE GROUND. GRAVITY PULLS THE STRING STRAIGHT DOWN.
A
B

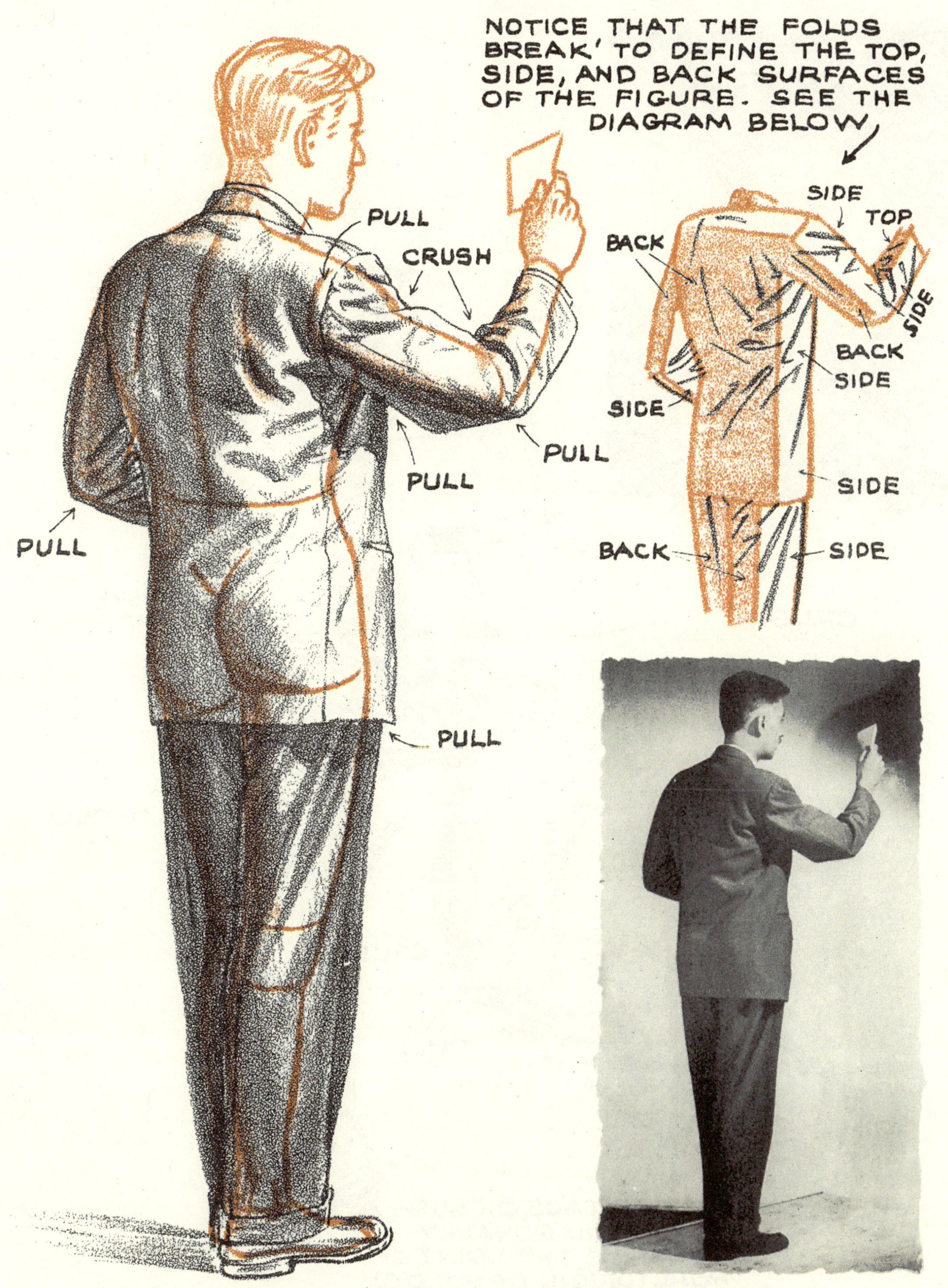
NOTICE THAT THE FOLDS 'BREAK' TO DEFINE THE TOP, SIDE, AND BACK SURFACES OF THE FIGURE. SEE THE DIAGRAM BELOW
PULL
CRUSH
PULL
PULL
PULL
PULL
PULL
SIDE
TOP
BACK
SIDE
BACK
SIDE
SIDE
SIDE
BACK
SIDE

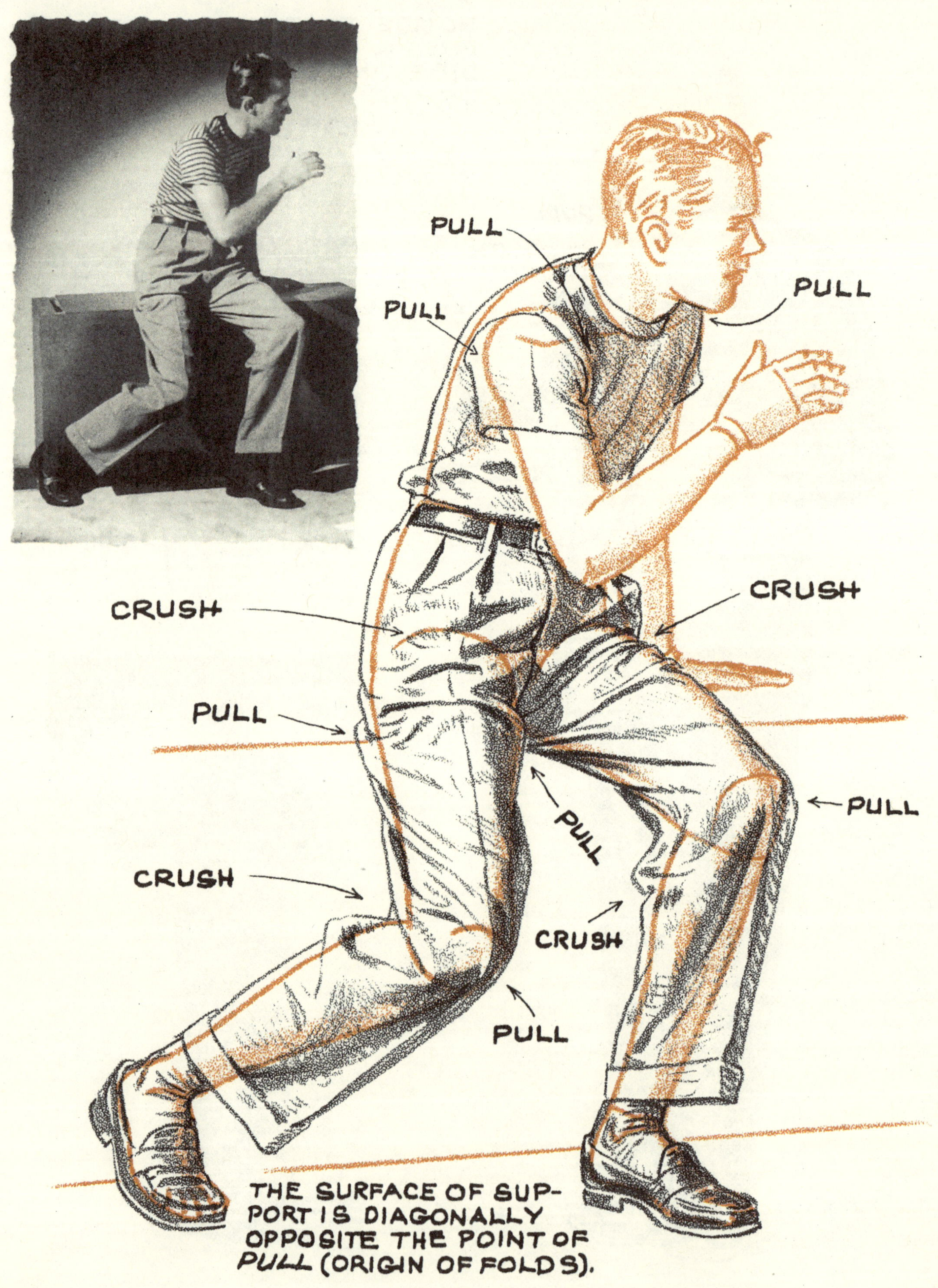
PULL
PULL
PULL
CRUSH
CRUSH
PULL
PULL
PULL
CRUSH
CRUSH
PULL
THE SURFACE OF SUP-
PORT IS DIAGONALLY
OPPOSITE THE POINT OF
PULL (ORIGIN OF FOLDS).

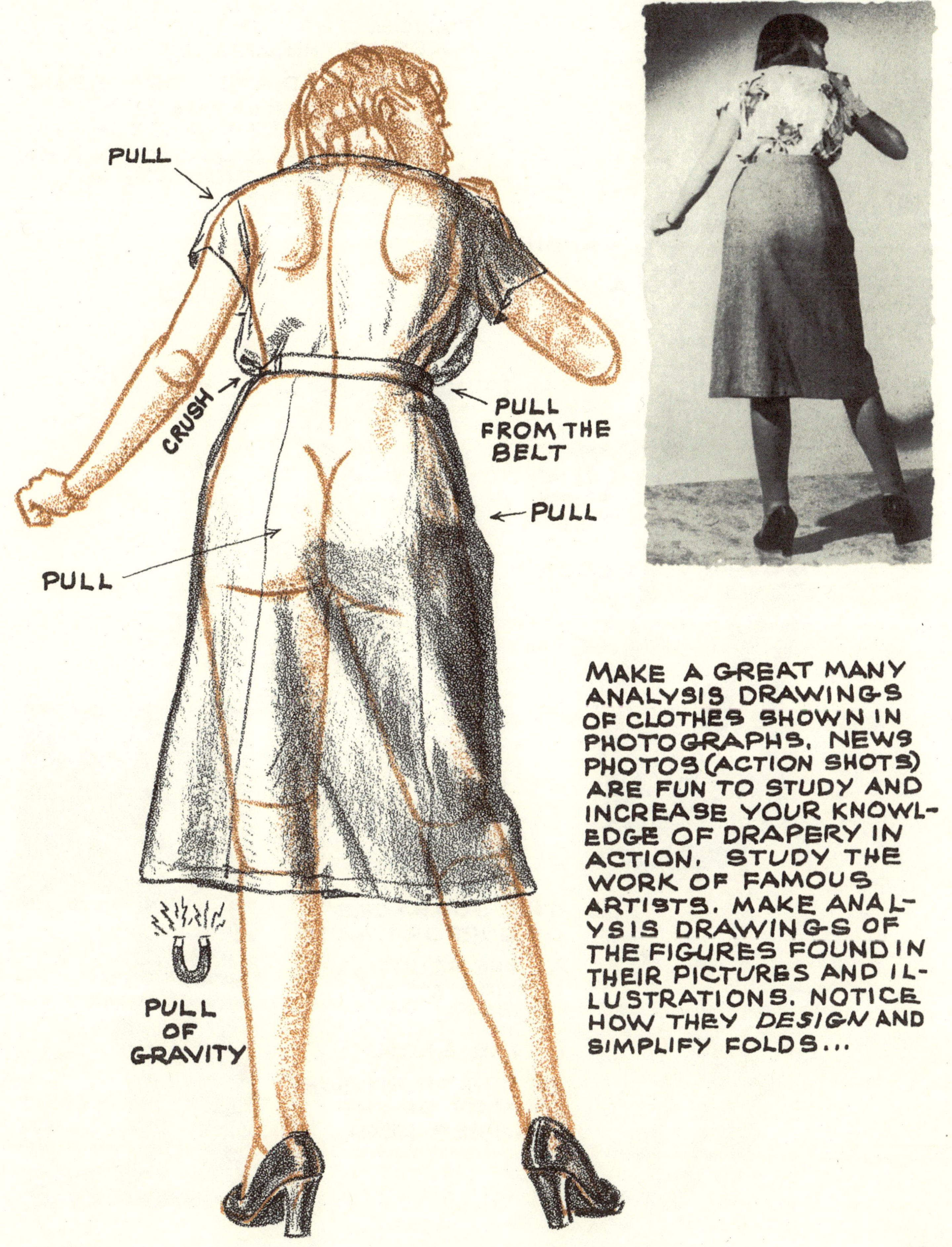

MAKE A GREAT MANY ANALYSIS DRAWINGS OF CLOTHES SHOWN IN PHOTOGRAPHS. NEWS PHOTOS (ACTION SHOTS) ARE FUN TO STUDY AND INCREASE YOUR KNOWLEDGE OF DRAPERY IN ACTION. STUDY THE WORK OF FAMOUS ARTISTS. MAKE ANALYSIS DRAWINGS OF THE FIGURES FOUND IN THEIR PICTURES AND ILLUSTRATIONS. NOTICE HOW THEY *DESIGN* AND SIMPLIFY FOLDS...

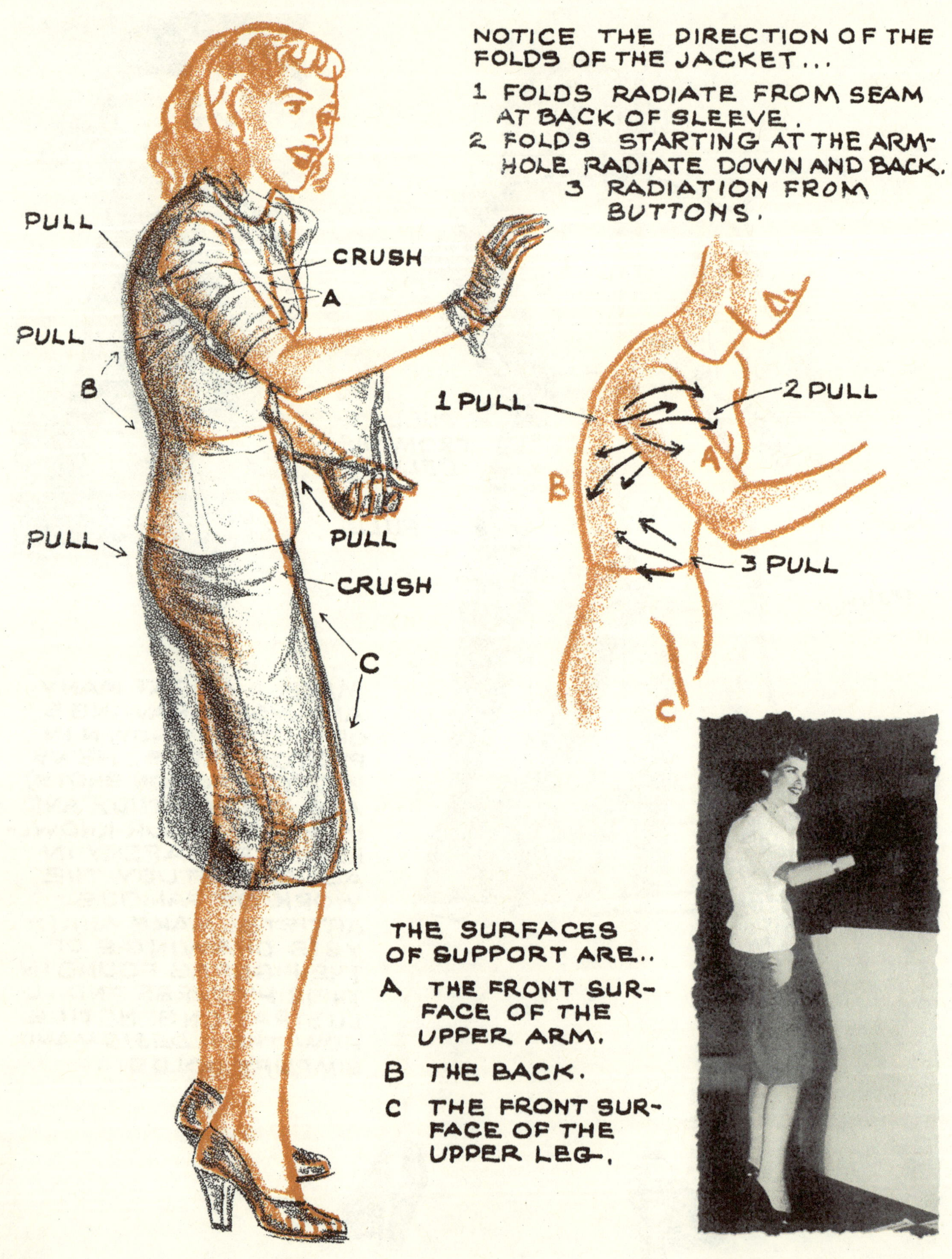
NOTICE THE DIRECTION OF THE FOLDS OF THE JACKET...
1 FOLDS RADIATE FROM SEAM AT BACK OF SLEEVE.
2 FOLDS STARTING AT THE ARM-HOLE RADIATE DOWN AND BACK.
3 RADIATION FROM BUTTONS.
PULL
CRUSH
A
PULL
B
PULL
PULL
CRUSH
C
1 PULL
2 PULL
A
B
3 PULL
C
THE SURFACES OF SUPPORT ARE..
A THE FRONT SURFACE OF THE UPPER ARM.
B THE BACK.
C THE FRONT SURFACE OF THE UPPER LEG.

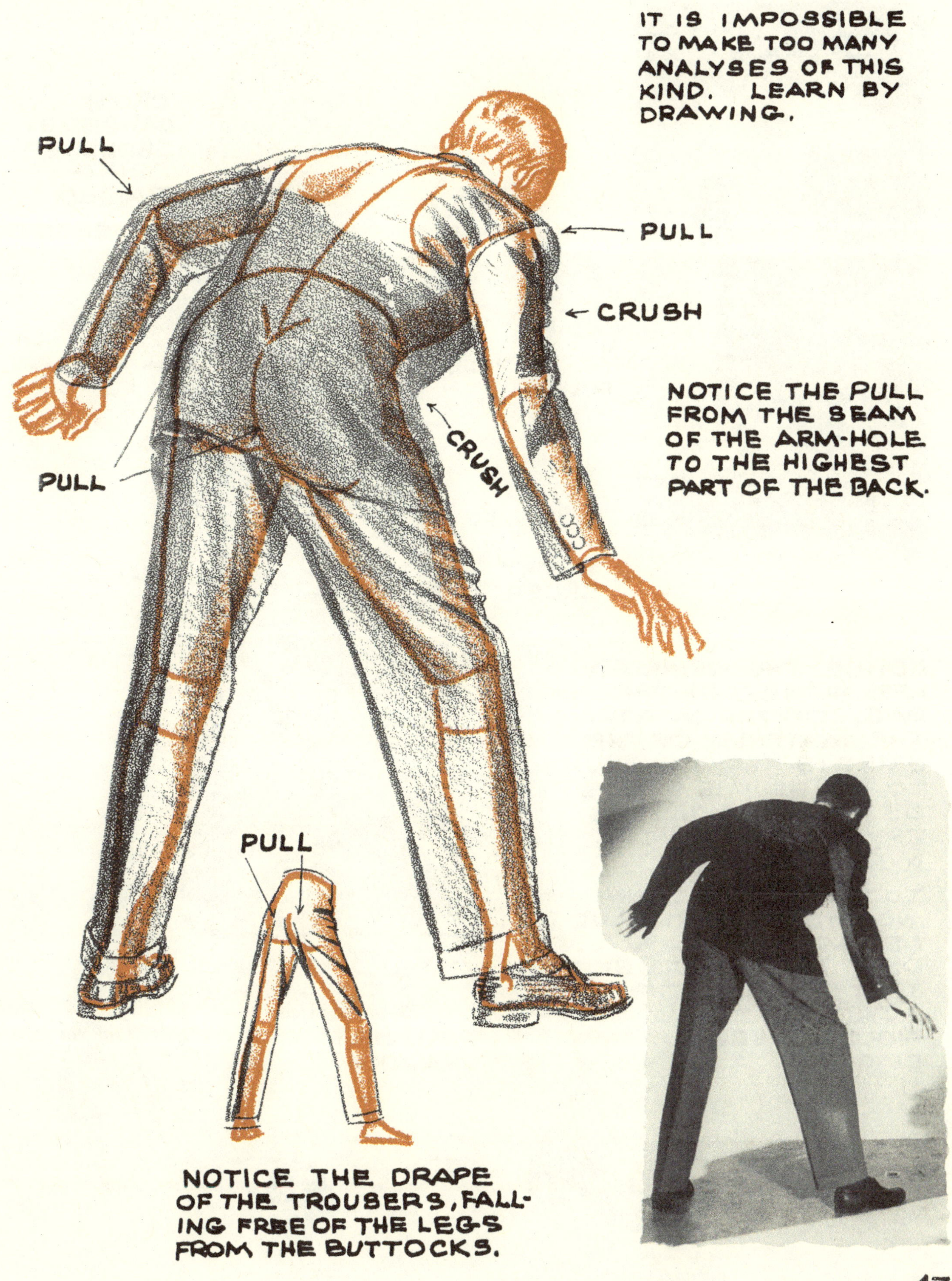
IT IS IMPOSSIBLE TO MAKE TOO MANY ANALYSES OF THIS KIND. LEARN BY DRAWING.
PULL
PULL
CRUSH
NOTICE THE PULL FROM THE SEAM OF THE ARM-HOLE TO THE HIGHEST PART OF THE BACK.
CRUSH
PULL
PULL
NOTICE THE DRAPE OF THE TROUSERS, FALLING FREE OF THE LEGS FROM THE BUTTOCKS.

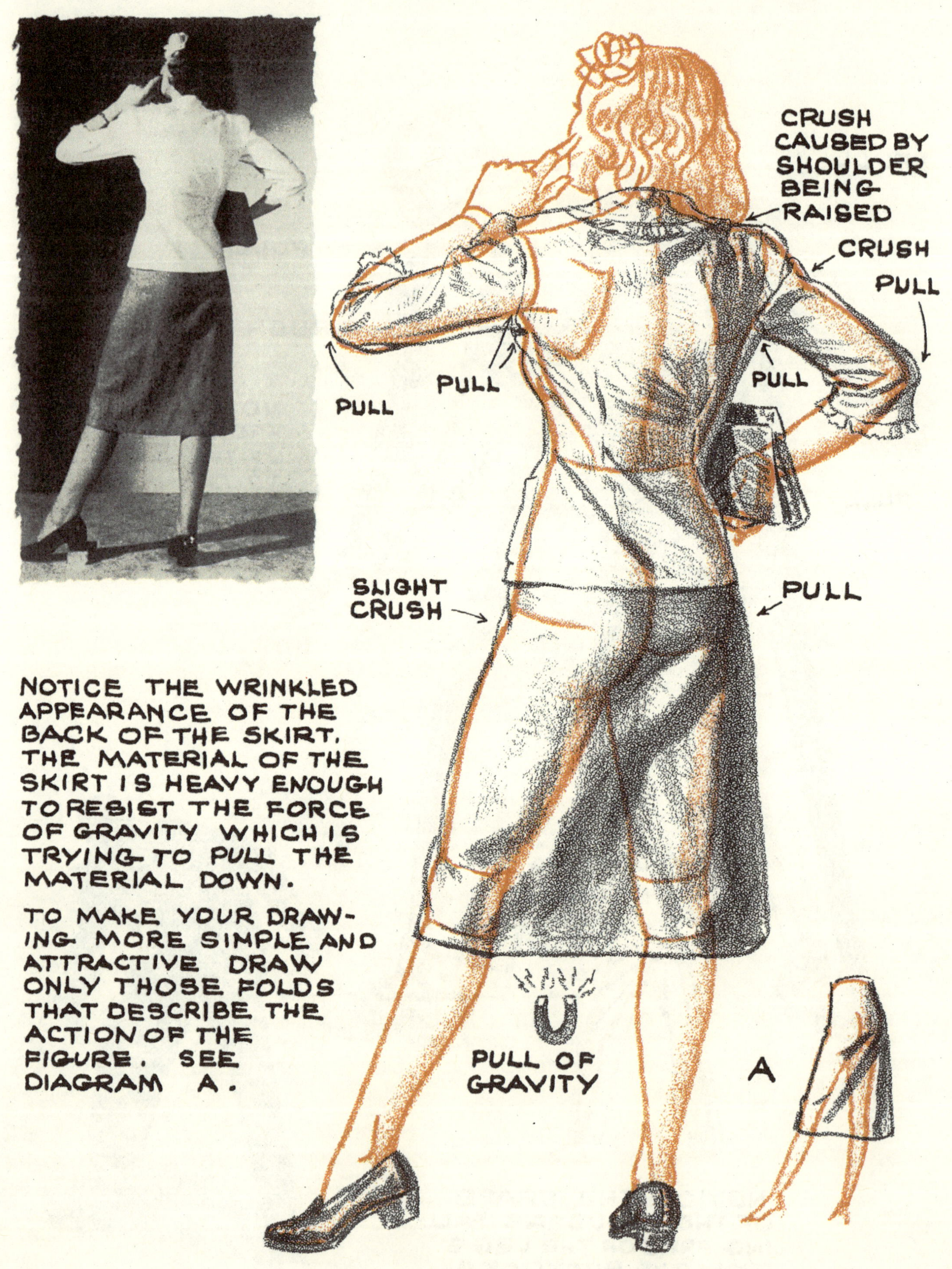

NOTICE THE WRINKLED APPEARANCE OF THE BACK OF THE SKIRT. THE MATERIAL OF THE SKIRT IS HEAVY ENOUGH TO RESIST THE FORCE OF GRAVITY WHICH IS TRYING TO PULL THE MATERIAL DOWN.

TO MAKE YOUR DRAWING MORE SIMPLE AND ATTRACTIVE DRAW ONLY THOSE FOLDS THAT DESCRIBE THE ACTION OF THE FIGURE. SEE DIAGRAM A.